A GENERAL'S LAST CALL

George C. Marshall
as Secretary of Defense
1950–51

Wayne C. Thompson

MARINER
PUBLISHING

3 5 7 9 10 8 6 4 2

Library of Congress Control Number: 2020912104

A General's Last Call
Wayne C. Thompson

p. cm.
1. Biography & Autobiography: Military
2. History: Military – Korean War
3. History: Military – United States

I. Thompson, Wayne 1943– II. Title.
ISBN 13: 978-0-9992885-9-7 (softcover : alk. paper)

Edited by Judy Rogers and Karen Bowen
Design and Layout by Karen Bowen

Mariner Publishing
An imprint of
Mariner Media, Inc.
131 West 21st Street
Buena Vista, VA 24416
Tel: 540-264-0021
www.marinermedia.com

Printed in the United States of America

This book is printed on acid-free paper meeting the requirements of the American Standard for Permanence of Paper for Printed Library Materials.

A GENERAL'S LAST CALL

TO SUSIE, JULIET, AND KATIE

Contents

Acknowledgments

I COULD NOT HAVE WRITTEN THIS BOOK WITHOUT THE GEORGE C. Marshall Foundation in Lexington, Virginia. I was given complete access to its library's rich holdings of documents and photographs. It provided me with a quiet place to work and to store my materials. The head librarians were always ready to assist me. Paul Barron offered me the opportunity to write the first book exclusively devoted to Marshall's last official assignment: as secretary of defense. He also taught me how to navigate the foundation's files. Jeffrey Kozak, who left to become the Virginia Military Institute's archivist, was ever ready to help me hunt materials and solve computer problems. Melissa Davis was indispensable in tracking down and preparing photos in the library's abundant photo files, which have enriched this work. The photos in this book are from George C. Marshall Foundation, unless otherwise noted. Mark A. Stoler, the editor of Volume 7 of the Marshall Papers, which were used heavily in this book, read the entire manuscript and offered valuable advice and suggestions for improvement. This study would never have seen the light of day without the support of Andy Wolfe, the president of Mariner Publishing. Karen Bowen was an excellent and demanding editor.

CHAPTER ONE

Marshall Becomes
Secretary of Defense

IN JANUARY 1949, A SIXTY-EIGHT-YEAR-OLD GENERAL GEORGE C.
Marshall stepped down as secretary of state after an
extraordinarily productive two years in office. In a divided and
changing post-war world, he had helped prevent Greece from
falling under Communist rule; support the resulting Truman
Doctrine, which offered assistance to countries threatened by
Communism; announce and implement the Marshall Plan,
which lifted the European allies out of poverty and hopelessness;
break the Berlin blockade; and lay the foundation stone of
NATO, which came into existence three months later when the
Washington Treaty was signed on April 4, 1949. His and his
country's standing in the eyes of its allies was at its highest.

This was demonstrated four years later on June 2, 1953, when
he represented the United States at the coronation of Queen
Elizabeth II in Westminster Abbey. This was the first time he
witnessed the crowning of a sovereign. He had written a letter
of condolence to the young queen upon the death of her father,
George VI. She wrote back that "I know that the King very
much enjoyed meeting you, and I remember so well when you
came here during the war."

He was accompanied by his wife (who was not invited to the ceremony in the Abbey), Chief Justice Earl Warren, and General Omar N. Bradley. His assigned seat was in row one of the first pew, the most honored seat for visiting dignitaries. After entering the church, he took the long walk up the corridor to his place. Marshall recalled Prime Minister Winston S. Churchill passing him on the way to the altar and then pausing, "he dignified me in the Abbey by turning out of the procession to shake hands with me after he had reached the dais." Field Marshal Montgomery and General Alan Brooke also defied protocol by leaving their places in the procession and going to Marshall to shake his hand. Bradley remembered that the attendees rose to their feet. Puzzled, Marshall looked around to see what dignitary had entered the Abbey and saw that he was the reason for such a display.

He was the only member of the American delegation to be invited to the post-coronation events. In a letter to President Harry S. Truman, he wrote: "I received a very gracious and warm welcome on all occasions and was particularly favored in the seating at the great banquets…was, I think, the only commoner so honored."[1] In December 1953, he became the first professional soldier to be awarded the Nobel Peace Prize.

By 1950, the aging general was exhausted by the burdens he had borne in the preceding decade. A third of his days as Secretary of State had been spent at international conferences. He was also weakened by the consequences of an operation on December 7, 1948, to have his right kidney removed. It slowed him down, robbed him of energy, and made him more vulnerable to fevers. He estimated that he had had only nineteen

---

1   Forest C. Pogue, *George C. Marshall: Statesman, 1945–1959*, pp. 500–502. See Debi and Irwin Unger with Stanley Hirshson, *George Marshall: A Biography*, p. 460. No British description of the coronation mentions the audience standing to honor Marshall's presence. This inclines a few scholars to be skeptical about certain aspects of this story.

days off since war had broken out in Europe in 1939, when he had assumed the post of General of the Army.

Retirement had thus far always eluded him. He had retired from the country's highest military command on November 26, 1945, after more than forty-three years of service in the United States Army. A grateful President Harry S. Truman awarded Marshall his only wartime decoration, a second Oak Leaf Cluster to go with his Distinguished Service Medal from the First World War. He read the much-quoted words from the official citation: "In a war unparalleled in magnitude and horror, millions of Americans gave their country outstanding service. General of the Army George C. Marshall gave it victory."[2]

Truman had known Marshall from the beginning of the Second World War. After starting his second Senatorial term on January 3, 1941, Truman had decided that he could best serve his country as a soldier. He believed he had the necessary military background. He had been a field artillery reserve captain in France during the First World War. In the spring of 1917, feeling "all patriotic," as he remembered, he had helped organize a new artillery battery in his native Missouri. His fellow National Guardsmen elected him as one of their officers.

In the night of March 29, 1918, his unit shipped out to Brest, on France's North Atlantic coast. On August 17, 1918, after several months of training, the 129th Field Artillery moved out by rail to the Vosges Mountains in Alsace, where his unit first engaged the enemy. Truman's battery was then ordered to move to the Argonne Forest in preparation for the largest military action in American history, the Meuse-Argonne offensive. Moving 600,000 men, 3,000 artillery pieces, 90,000 horses and trucks, and supplies almost 100 miles by night was a logistical nightmare. The surreptitious nocturnal redeployment had been

---

2   Mark A. Stoler, *George C. Marshall: Soldier-Statesman of the American Century*, pp. 142, 173.

worked out by a brilliant soldier on General John J. Pershing's staff: Brevet Colonel George C. Marshall. In the ensuing battle Truman's regiment suffered 129 battlefield casualties. His Battery D counted only three wounded, one of whom subsequently died. On April 9, 1919, Truman and his men sailed for home on the former German ocean liner, the *Zeppelin*. After the Great War from 1919 to 1940, Captain Truman trained reserve officers in camps and night schools.

Considering himself a seasoned experienced soldier, Truman went to General Marshall and told him he wished to resign from the Senate and enter the armed service as a field artillery colonel and instructor. As Truman remembered the exchange, after hearing that Truman was fifty-six years of age, Marshall "pulled his reading glasses down on his nose, grinned at me and said, We don't need old stiffs like you—this will be a young man's war." Truman admitted: "He was right, of course, but it hurt my feelings and I decided to do something for the war effort on a constructive basis."[3]

No sooner had Marshall arrived at his home in Leesburg, Virginia, at war's end than President Truman called him the very next day, November 27, 1945, and asked him to undertake an important but difficult mission to China, which was on the precipice of anarchy and civil war. His assignment was to find a way for the Communists and Nationalists to stop their fighting and to forge a unified country and army. Marshall

---

3   For Truman's First World War experience, see David McCullough, *Truman*, pp. 102–38. Robert H. Ferrell, ed., *The Autobiography of Harry S. Truman*, pp. 74–75. For Marshall's preference for a promotion system that favored young men, see Mark A. Stoler, ed., *The Papers of George Catlett Marshall*, Vol. 7, "The Man of the Age," October 1, 1949–October 16, 1959, document 361. Hereafter referred to as *Marshall Papers*, Vol. 7. References to information in the numbered documents will be cited by document numbers. Explanatory text written by the editors will be cited by page numbers.

*Marshall and Mao Zedong during the former's
mission to China, March 1946.*

immediately accepted and left almost immediately. He wrote
General Douglas MacArthur, whom he had known, served
and commanded during most of his career: "My retirement
was of rather short duration."[4] Despite his year-long efforts
and almost three hundred meetings, the mission foundered on
Communist intransigence and Nationalist incompetence and
corruption. Unaware that America's power was not unlimited
in Asia, political enemies in and out of Congress accused
him for years of "losing China." A year later, in January 1947,
Truman brought Marshall home to replace the unpopular
James Byrnes as secretary of state. He agreed to take charge of
the State Department, which had become the key actor in US
foreign policy.

---

4   Stoler, *Marshall*, p. 145.

He served two years until January 1949. His retirement was relatively well funded after Congress passed legislation granting full salaries and benefits to the nine generals and admirals, including Marshall, who had achieved five-star rank. Congress also made that five-star rank permanent.[5] Rather than choose pleasant retirement in his Leesburg garden, which he loved, he took on a further responsibility that seemed to offer him a more relaxing way to serve his country: as the chairman of the American Red Cross. The organization was under fire because of a feeling that it was being run by so few people. Truman concluded that the Red Cross needed a gifted and respected leader who had previously not been involved in the perpetual infighting.

Marshall agreed to the offer and threw himself into his new responsibilities. He worked to smooth out the rivalries and disputes within the organization, and he traveled widely in the early months of his assignment, totaling thirty-five thousand miles in autos, trains, and planes. It was claimed that he had worn out several subordinates by the time he left. The outbreak of the Korean War on June 25, 1950, enhanced the importance of its Blood Bank drive. But the drums of war in the summer of 1950 made it unlikely that a man with Marshall's leadership talent, experience, political savvy, and familiarity with the nation's military leaders could remain forever in a humanitarian organization like the Red Cross, despite the good work he and it did.

NOMINATION AND CONFIRMATION

At 4:00 a.m. on June 25, 1950, North Korean troops equipped with Soviet weaponry attacked South Korea, swarming across the 38th Parallel. There were no US combat troops there to slow them down or repel them. The last remaining combat team had been withdrawn the end of June 1949, a year earlier, in an

---

5   Pogue, *Marshall*, p. 415.

overall reduction of American conventional forces in Asia. On May 29, 1949, *The New York Times* had run a story headlined "U.S. to Quit Korea in July," and that happened. A half of a year later, on January 12, 1950, Secretary of State Dean Acheson had inadvertently said in a speech to the National Press Club that Korea was out of America's defense perimeter.[6] There was understandable confusion whether the US would ever mount a defense of South Korea. Nevertheless, this unprovoked attack was immediately perceived as directly affecting US and free world interests. The situation went from serious to disastrous, as the North Koreans drove back the South Korean defenders into a tiny perimeter around the southern port city of Pusan. Plans were hastily made to evacuate US civilians and military advisers.[7]

A woefully unprepared United States turned to the recently created United Nations for help. Thanks to the fact that the Soviet Union had absented itself from the Security Council in protest against the granting of China's seat to the Nationalist regime in Formosa, not to the Communist government in Peking (Beijing). Three resolutions were passed on June 25, June 27, and July 7, 1950, requesting troops to be placed under a unified commander to be named by the United States. President Truman appointed General of the Army Douglas MacArthur, then commander of the Allied occupation forces in Japan. Ultimately seventeen nations sent troops to defend South Korea.[8]

By September 1950, the president had concluded that a new secretary was needed in the nascent department of defense. He

---

6   Carl W. Borklund, *Men of the Pentagon: From Forrestal to McNamara*, p. 98.

7   *Marshall Papers*, Vol. 7, p. 125 and document 103.

8   Unger, *Marshall*, p. 459. When Marshall became defense secretary on September 21, 1950, eleven countries had already agreed to support the UN effort. Pogue, *Marshall*, p. 452. See in a later chapter in this book a more detailed discussion of the outbreak of war in Korea.

wrote that Louis A. Johnson "offended every member of the cabinet" and "never missed an opportunity to say mean things about my personal staff."[9] In such a crisis as Korea, the newly created department of defense needed the right kind of leader. A good secretary of defense had to have the confidence of the president and be able to work with him. Since national security had come to mean much more than merely military power, he had to be able to cooperate harmoniously with the secretary of state and with other high national security officials, most of whom were civilian. He had to have the trust of the military and to be able to establish and maintain a high level of morale on the part of its leaders and the almost 1.5 million soldiers, sailors, and airmen on active duty. He also had to understand how the bewildering federal bureaucracy works, including that of the military services. He should be able to manage a rapidly growing defense department that by 1950 had swelled to more than 2,700 personnel, mostly civilians, serving under the secretary.

The nation was at war, so the secretary had to be a good crisis manager with a firm grasp of strategy at the highest level and, since 1945, of the role of nuclear weapons in that strategy. He had to understand the budgetary process and be experienced in dealing with Congress. He must be able to win the approval and support of a majority of the nation's legislators. Finally he had to possess effective diplomatic skills and be trusted and respected by America's many allies.[10]

In his ground-breaking study *Soldier and State*, Harvard Professor Samuel Huntington listed the following as desirable characteristics of a secretary of defense: he should have experience, be a man of respect, be a man of dedication, acting and thinking purely in terms of the office, should be at the end

---

9   Pogue, *Marshall,* p. 421.

10   Roger R. Trask and Alfred Goldberg, *The Department of Defense 1947–1997: Organization and Leaders,* pp. 12, 130.

point not a stepping stone in a public career, and be a man of policy. "His greatest needs are breadth, wisdom, insight, and, above all, judgment. He is neither operator, administrator, nor commander. But he is policy maker."[11]

President Truman knew just the person who would fit this awesome job description: General Marshall, as he was called by everybody at the time, including by the president, the secretary of state and his own staff. Although the president was not yet ready to fire Johnson, Truman and his daughter, Margaret, drove across the Potomac to Marshall's Leesburg home on July 4, 1950. The president told the general about his difficulties with Johnson. Marshall let the president know that he was enjoying retirement. But he confessed in a letter to his goddaughter, Rose Page Wilson: "When the President comes down and sits under our oaks and tells me of his difficulties, he has me at a disadvantage." Marshall noted that he was a soldier and would do his duty for a limited time. Truman asked him to ponder the prospect of returning to his nation's service.[12]

In August 1950, Marshall and his wife were vacationing at a resort at Huron Mountain in northern Michigan. He was summoned from the camp where they were staying to the closest public telephone at a nearby country store a half of an hour away. The president was on the line. There were many curious locals in the store who had heard the word that the president was calling. They were carefully listening to what the famous general would say. Aware that he was being overheard, Marshall was "unusually abrupt in giving his assent," as Truman once told Dean Acheson. Would he consider becoming secretary of defense? He was asked please to think about it and come see him in Washington when

---

11   Samuel P. Huntington, *The Soldier and the State: The Theory and Politics of Civil-Military Relations*, pp. 453–55.

12   Ed Cray, *General of the Army: George C. Marshall, Soldier and Statesman*, p. 684.

he was back in town. Since Truman had gotten Marshall to agree to undertake the China mission before Mrs. Marshall could be informed, he was not asking for an immediate answer.[13]

After returning to the capital, Marshall visited the president on September 6 in Blair House across the street from the White House, which was being restored. The general informed Truman that he would accept the post, subject to certain conditions. One was that it be only about six months in duration. He later agreed to extend this to late June 1951. But since his pet project, Universal Military Training (UMT), was being considered in Congress in June, he subsequently agreed to remain in office until September 12, 1951.

His second important condition was that Robert Lovett, his former under-secretary of state and an admired and well-liked Wall Street banker and public servant, be his deputy secretary of defense and take over as secretary when Marshall retired. He gave a gentle reminder to the president that "I want you to think about the fact that my appointment may reflect upon your Administration. They are still charging me with the downfall of Chiang's government in China. I want to help, not hurt you." Of course, Truman had already thought about this. But he was nevertheless touched by the general's honesty while being offered one of the most influential jobs in the world. The president wrote to his wife: "Can you think of anyone else saying that? I can't and he's of the great." President Truman accepted all his terms.[14]

In the acrimonious political environment of the day, Marshall's senatorial confirmation as secretary of defense did not go as smoothly as the administration had anticipated. Republicans were in an angry mood after having not only lost

---

13   Pogue, *Marshall*, p. 420. Trask, *DOD*, p. 96. Dean Acheson, *Present at the Creation: My Years in the State Department*, p. 441.

14   Cray, *General*, pp. 684-85. Pogue, *Marshall*, p. 422. See *Marshall Papers*, Vol. 7, documents 79, 81, 86 and p. 155.

*Undersecretary of Defense Robert Lovett with
President Truman and Marshall.*

the presidential election in 1948, but had lost their control over
Congress as well. Therefore, the kind of unanimous confirmation
Marshall had received as the nominee to become secretary of
state in 1947 did not happen this time.

There were several obstacles that could potentially have
derailed his appointment. The first was a law prohibiting any
person who had been a commissioned officer on active duty
within the previous ten years from serving as secretary of
defense. This was a legitimate concern and had been written
into the National Security Act of 1947. The rationale for this
was the long-standing principle of civilian supremacy over the
military. In the confirmation hearing before the Committee on
Armed Services United States Senate on September 19, 1950,
Senator Harry P. Cain, Republican from Washington, explained
his own dilemma by describing Marshall as "one of the most

distinguished persons in the annals of American military history." Nevertheless, "in my opinion, America will not solve her problems by endeavoring to find a soldier, old or young, to carry the burdens which ought to be borne and conquered by civilian citizens."

Cain ended his statement graciously, offering Marshall his assistance "in every conceivable way" in carrying out his burdens. "Upon the assumption that you will shortly become America's Secretary of Defense, I wish you well, sound health, and a long life." The general was asked about his health, and he answered: "I arrived here direct from Walter Reed Hospital....They have been working on me for 2 days, and they say the machinery is all right."[15]

Marshall agreed with this principle, noting in his confirmation that he had changed his own opinion over a forty-three-year military career. Asked what he thought of civilian control, he answered that when he was a second lieutenant, he believed "we would never get anywhere in the Army unless a soldier was Secretary of War." But as he grew a little older and "served through some of our military history, particularly the Philippine Insurrection, I came to the fixed conclusion that he should never be a soldier."[16] Later during the Second World War, when he had the authority to do practically everything he wished, he conscientiously informed and counseled the civilian secretary of war, Henry Stimson.[17] *The Washington Post* was correct in asserting that Marshall was a military man with a civilian mind. In the end, it was not possible to show that the actions of a military officer necessarily reflected "the inherently

---

15 See Marshall's Confirmation Hearing in *Hearing Before the Committee on Armed Services United States Senate, September 19, 1950,* pp. 2–3, 24. See *Marshall Papers,* Vol. 7, document 103.

16 Hearing, p. 8.

17 Borklund, *Men of Pentagon,* p. 112.

dangerous qualities of a military mind." Examining the specifics of a man like Marshall, "the threat of militarization rapidly evaporated."[18]

The nominee was asked a variety of questions, loaded and otherwise. He evaded many on the grounds that he had been out of the loop for a while and had to inform himself and confer with the president and secretary of state. He was asked if he favored rearming Germany as a NATO ally. Marshall answered that he had not yet decided, but he quickly became an ardent supporter of this after taking office. He confirmed that he had "initiated most of the unity proposals [for the armed services] while I was Chief of Staff" and that he had helped in reorganizing the War Department in February 1942. "I have been an ardent advocate of unifying the services. I suffered from the lack of unification throughout the war." He also said he supported the establishment of the National Security Council (NSC) created in 1947 by the National Security Act.[19]

He showed his usual courage, responding to questions about Secretary of State Dean Acheson. He had been Marshall's first deputy secretary of state and in some minds had become the embodiment of a series of failures in US foreign policy, including the Communist victory in China and the ongoing war in Korea. He explained to the senators that "the Secretary of State is the natural leader up to the President in the matter of our international relationships." It is the job of the secretary of defense "to make clear what the situation is or would be with regard to our Armed Forces." Foreshadowing his practice as defense secretary of facilitating regular meetings between state and defense department officials at all levels, he noted that informal conversations taking place all the time are as important as a formal meeting. He refused to answer one written inquiry

---

18   Pogue, *Marshall*, p 423. Huntington, *Soldier*, p. 360.

19   Hearing, pp. 4, 6, 9.

for assurance that he would "not be dominated by or carry out the policies of Secretary of State Dean Acheson, who will not turn his back on Alger Hiss." Often dogged by critics for allegedly having "lost China," Marshall explained that his job during his unsuccessful mission to China was to stop the fighting and bring about the cessation of conflict.[20]

Some questions were asked to score political points with the voters back home. They turned nasty and provided an unpleasant preview of some of the outrageous charges directed against Marshall a year later by Senator Joseph McCarthy, Republican of Wisconsin. Senator William Jenner of Indiana inquired about his whereabouts the night before the Pearl Harbor attack, insinuating yet again that President Franklin D. Roosevelt had ordered him to go to some secret location, evidently in a plot to do harm to the United States. Marshall said he was fairly positive he had been home that night.[21] Why had he not protested against the agreements reached at Tehran, Yalta, and Potsdam, "which handed half the world on a silver platter to Stalin"? Marshall answered that he had "read about them first in the press afterward, so far as they were disclosed." Another written question asked whom he was trying to protect by not writing memoirs. Did he "favor surrendering American sovereignty into the hands of an international super state and the turning of American Armed Forces into a permanent foreign legion"? An amused Marshall responded: "That pretty well covers the water front. No, I am not in favor of that."[22] The committee voted to approve Marshall's nomination by a vote of ten to two.

---

20   Hearing, pp. 21, 24. Alger Hiss was a State Department official suspected of ties with Communists.

21   Pogue, *Marshall,* pp. 425–26.

22   Hearing, pp. 20, 24.

The question on amending the 1947 National Security Act to permit a recently serving military officer to be secretary of defense went to both chambers on September 15, 1950. With lower house elections only two months away, exaggerated rhetoric filled the air. Representative Dewey Short of Missouri got fellow Republicans out of their seats by calling Marshall "a catspaw and a pawn" who had gotten Truman's call in the Michigan country store in order "to bail out desperate men who are in a hole." The House of Representatives added a stipulation to the law that only Marshall was to enjoy the exception. This amendment was also accepted by the Senate. One hundred ninety-three House Democrats joined twenty-seven Republicans—including Richard Nixon of California and Jacob Javits of New York—to pass the amendment 220 to 105.[23]

There was some opposition in the Senate to Marshall's appointment. Senator Robert Taft of Ohio, supported by some other Senators, expressed the opinion that a vote for Marshall would be a vote for Communism in the Far East and for approval of Acheson's flawed policies in China, Formosa, and Korea. But the prize for preposterous allegations went to Senator Jenner, who faced reelection in two years. Delivering a scathing speech to his stony-faced colleagues in what *New York Times* correspondent William S. White described as "shouts and half-screams," Jenner contended that the Democratic Party had been captured from the inside and was hastening the country to its destruction. The Truman administration was desperate and was attempting to cover up "its bloody tracks of treason." His most unforgettable lines were these: "General Marshall is not only willing, he is eager to play the role of a front man for traitors. The truth is [that] this is no new role for him, for General George C. Marshall is a living lie." Not finished yet, Jenner went on to describe Marshall as "an errand boy, a front man, a stooge, or a conspirator for

---

23   Pogue, *Marshall,* p. 426. *Marshall Papers,* Vol. 7, document 99.

this Administration's crazy assortment of collectivist cutthroat crackpots and Communist fellow-travelling appeasers." This was too much even for most of his stunned GOP party comrades, who distanced themselves from him.[24] At the end of the debate, forty-two Democrats teamed up with fifteen Republicans to approve Marshall's appointment fifty-seven to eleven.

The waiver in Marshall's case was popular. The *Minneapolis Tribune* published a poll on December 3, 1950, showing that 70 percent of Minnesotans favored a military man as defense secretary in both war and peace; 80 percent (83 percent of WWII veterans) were in favor of Marshall in that post. Not until sixty-seven years later, in January 2017, was a retired officer, Marine four-star General James Mattis, appointed defense secretary. The time limit had already been reduced from ten to seven years. Only three years out of active duty, Mattis sailed easily through the Senate ratification process.[25]

After learning of his confirmation, Marshall left his office at Red Cross headquarters in Washington and was chauffeured in his ancient Studebaker to his new and former place of employment: the Pentagon. When he arrived at the secretary's office, he said, "Guess we have to go through the oath business." The last thing on his mind was a grandiose swearing-in ceremony. The outgoing deputy secretary, Steven Early, who would soon be replaced by Robert Lovett, sent for a photographer and called in the deputy general counsel to officiate. One of Marshall's assistants remarked: "You could count on two hands the people who knew what was in process. When this ten-minute affair ended, the Joint Chiefs were called in and we were in business."[26]

---

24 Pogue, *Marshall*, pp. 426–27. Stoler, *Marshall*, pp. 182–83.

25 "Toughness and Restraint at Defense," *The New York Times*, January 13, 2017.

26 Borklund, *Men of Pentagon*, p. 101.

Marshall sworn in as Secretary of Defense, September 21, 1950.

On September 21, 1950, George C. Marshall became America's third secretary of defense. This was the third time he was recalled to duty since he retired as Chief of Staff in November 1945. He was assuming control over a gigantic organization created in 1947 and still in its infancy. As Samuel P. Huntington described it in the 1950s, it was "still young as government offices go. Its powers and prerogatives have not been defined and frozen into a fixed pattern. It is still primarily the man who shapes the office rather than the office which shapes the man. Personality and tradition are more important than statutes."[27]

But it was already becoming one of the federal government's main centers of decision and power. On that first day, he had difficulties figuring out how to use the three buttons on the side

---

27   Huntington, *Soldier*, p. 453.

of his desk. One was to call the deputy secretary, another for the top military aide, and a third for his secretary. He had all three rushing into his office simultaneously every quarter of an hour until he learned not to let the arm of his chair bump into all three buttons at once.[28] This was an early reminder of how difficult it had become to be boss of the immense department of defense, which had already grown to be the executive branch's biggest organization by far.

UNIFICATION OF THE ARMED FORCES

The United States had fought the Second World War with a complicated makeshift defense apparatus that persuaded all the nation's leaders that major reform, especially the unification of the different branches of service, had to be undertaken. At the same time they were all aware that the challenges of the total war they were waging precluded any serious tinkering until peace had been achieved. Discussions began in 1944, but they invariably stirred controversy. Marshall, as Army Chief of Staff, was in complete agreement on the need to unify the forces while giving the Army Air Corps, led by General H. H. "Hap" Arnold, independent status; "but not until after the war." President Roosevelt rebutted any call for unification by saying: "Let's win the war first." The de facto unified control that led to victory was forged on the field and through the successful cooperation of the military chiefs—Fleet Admiral William D. Leahy, Roosevelt's chief of staff, General of the Army Marshall as Army Chief of Staff, Fleet Admiral Ernest J. King, Chief of Naval Operations, and General Hap Arnold of the Army Air Force. All joined the deliberations. Their authority was rooted in the need for teamwork, not in law.[29]

---

28   Borklund, *Men of Pentagon*, p. 101.

29   Carl W. Borklund, *The Department of Defense*, pp. 19–20. Cray, *General*, p. 682.

As their war came to an end, Americans found the wartime arrangements faulty and in need of reform. Many were ad hoc and temporary. During the Second World War there existed a bewildering network of some seventy-five major service agencies and interdepartmental committees to attempt to coordinate the war effort. There was sufficient confusion during the struggle to remind the nation's leaders that having an effective and efficient multi-level organization is every bit as important as finding the right strategy to win the war. Some form of centralized control over military operations was clearly more effective than the kind of voluntary inter-service cooperation that existed at the outbreak of hostilities.[30]

The debate about whether and how to unify the different branches of service is about as old as the American republic itself. Article II, Section 2 of the constitution vests the singular right to direct the armed forces in one person: the president, who is the "Commander-in-Chief of the Army and Navy." For almost a decade the first president was assisted in military matters by a single person, the Secretary of War, who was selected to lead the War Department. After building a fleet to combat the marauding Barbary pirates in the Mediterranean, a Department of the Navy was created in 1798. For the next century and a half, the sole official who could settle disputes between these two often bickering departments was the president. Not until 1947, when a single secretary of defense was created, would the commander-in-chief have a single deputy for all military issues, the newly created office of secretary of defense.[31]

It took a long time to get to that point. Between 1921 and 1945, about fifty pieces of legislation calling for unification were submitted to Congress. All were defeated. In 1932, one of them

---

30   Steven L. Rearden, *The Formative Years, 1947–1950*, Vol. 1 of *History of the Office of the Secretary of Defense*, ed. Alfred Goldberg, pp. 16–17.

31   Borklund, *Department*, pp. 3–4.

actually reached the floor of the House of Representatives, but it was rejected by a vote of 153 to 135. The issue died down during the depression years of the 1930s, when Americans' attention was focused on more basic problems. But from 1943 to 1947 debate over the notion of uniting the forces and having a single military department was reignited.[32] Both the War and Navy departments had their staunch supporters on Capitol Hill. Suspicions and different strongly held beliefs prevented compromises from taking shape.

All discussions through World War II to the postwar years turned on the questions of how the services should relate with each other and whether aviation should have its own service, equal to the Army and Navy. The Navy dragged its heels the hardest. It feared that reform would mean the loss of its and the Marine Corps' air arms to a new and unified air force. A single civilian defense leader could downgrade the role of the Navy in general. The Marine Corps was deeply worried that it was destined to be completely swallowed up by the Army into one combined land force. Its fears were not quieted by remarks by Omar Bradley in October 1949 that "large-scale amphibious operations will never occur again. The first prize of any aggressor is Europe."[33] The Korean War helped convince doubters that the Marines had a crucial role to play in modern warfare.

The issue was moved to the forefront by President Truman, who put detailed recommendations on the table. After the enormous but largely necessary military expenditures during the war, he was determined to cut military spending drastically in the postwar era. As a senator during the war, he chaired the Senate Appropriations and Military Affairs Committees and the Special Committee to Investigate the National Defense Program. His insider's look at how the nation's treasure was

---

32   Borklund, *Department,* pp. 6–7.

33   Rearden, *Formative Years,* pp. 18–19. Borklund, *Men of Pentagon,* p. 98.

used to buy war materials shocked him: "appalling waste" and "numerous unnecessary duplications" were discovered in both the War and Navy departments. He was determined as president to eliminate "bureaucratic waste" and "overlapping jurisdictions." He concluded that the entire "antiquated defense setup" needed to be reformed from top to bottom.

As a candidate for the vice presidency in 1944, Truman had published an article in *Collier's* asserting that the only thing that could prevent such waste and inefficiency was "a single authority over everything that pertains to American safety." He put pressure on Secretary of the Navy James Forrestal and Secretary of War Robert P. Patterson to narrow their differences. But by the end of May 1946, they were still deadlocked over four contentious points: the creation of a single secretary that would lead the entire military establishment, whether a separate air force should have the same status as the Army and Navy, whether the Navy and Marines should retain their land-based air capability to support naval operations, and what the overall mission of the Marine Corps should be. In the fourteen months that followed, these issues would be resolved in the intensive debates and discussions that took place under encouragement and pressure from the president. This culminated in the president's signature on July 26, 1947, of the National Security Act. Congress changed its committee structure in early 1947 to adjust to unification by replacing in each house the separate committees on naval and military affairs with a unified committee on armed services.[34]

NATIONAL SECURITY ACT, 1947

The nation's experiences during the war had taught its leaders that their military establishment was only one part of the

---

34 Rearden, *Formative Years*, pp. 20–21. Doris M. Condit, *The Test of War, 1950–1953.* Vol. 2 of *History of the Office of the Secretary of Defense*, ed. Alfred Goldberg, p. 14.

country's overall security. In a world fundamentally changed by the war that had just been completed, not only would military organization have to be changed, but a larger more coherent military-political framework for national security policy would have to be devised. The heart of what emerged from the debate was unification of the forces.[35] But the National Security Act (NSA) also cemented civilian domination of the military. It changed the way foreign policy was formulated and how intelligence work should relate to that effort. Including its amendment in 1949, the NSA arguably constituted the most fundamental reform of the federal government since the country's founding. The resulting institutions continue to serve Americans in the twenty-first century.

Within the armed services, it was the Army that pressed for the most far-reaching change. Although he had his hands full with other responsibilities after the Second World War, Marshall supported unification of the forces. The Army had long advocated a single secretary of defense and a chief of staff or single military commander. The Navy opposed a single department while accepting a separate Air Force. Such an independent air arm enjoyed wide support in the military, Congress and the public. The Army Air Force (AAF) had played a visibly key role during the war and had already acquired near complete autonomy within the Army. In 1945, its 2.4 million airmen constituted 31 percent of the Army. Its size was three-fourths the total manpower of the Navy and five times larger than the Marine Corps. As for the latter, the Army was insistent that it would not constitute a second land army and should limit its activities to supporting the fleet. The war in Korea would put that Army policy to the test. In 1945, the United States had demonstrated in Japan that it was the only nation in the world at the time that possessed nuclear weapons. All three services

---

35   Trask, *DOD*, p. 3. Borklund, *Department*, p. 7.

insisted upon and won a share in the control and employment of those atomic weapons.[36] The resulting NSA legislation was, like most reforms, a compromise that did not completely satisfy anybody. It was a huge and controversial package that was debated by Congress for six months before approving it and passing it to the president for his signature. He immediately signed it on July 26, 1947.

The 1947 National Security Act provided for secretaries of the three military departments for the Army (the former War Department), Navy, and the newly separate Air Force. The service departments remained basically autonomous organizations and exercised control over their inner affairs. Each service secretary had the right, after informing the newly created secretary of defense, to appeal any decision of the latter to the Congress or president. Any powers and duties not specifically granted to the secretary of defense would accrue to the service secretaries. They were full members of the president's cabinet and had seats on the newly established National Security Council (NSC). The secretary of defense's authority was restricted further by forbidding him from establishing a "military staff."[37]

It was made clear that his authority was only to exercise "general direction, authority, and control" over the service departments. The word "general" was key. The service secretaries interpreted it to mean that the secretary of defense could deal with them only by means of cooperation, not directives.[38] Decisions could be reached only through discussion and mutual consent. As the first secretary of defense discovered, that was an exhausting and frustrating necessity that could not last.

---

36   Trask, *DOD*, pp. 4–7.

37   Rearden, *Formative Years*, p. 25.

38   William R. Kintner, *Forging a New Sword: A Study of the Department of Defense*, p. 26. C.W. Borklund called this contraption a "confederation." Borklund, *Department*, p. 45.

A "National Military Establishment (NME)" was created above the service departments. It was not defined clearly in the NSA and remained unsatisfactory and vague. A secretary of defense was established to be "the principal assistant to the President in all matters relating to the national security." This secretary should lay out "general policies and programs" for the NME, get rid of "unnecessary duplication or overlapping" and oversee and coordinate the preparation and implementation of the annual defense budget. It was precisely the budget that was the defense secretary's greatest power in his attempts to maintain unity and efficiency.[39]

The National Security Act created a Central Intelligence Agency (CIA) to replace the former Office of Strategic Services and Central Intelligence Group in order to "insure a sound and adequate intelligence base for the formulation and execution of national security policies." While it was designed to coordinate the government agencies' intelligence activities, all intelligence organizations already existing would continue their work as before. The act also created a National Security Resources Board (NSRB) whose purpose was to "advise the President concerning the coordination of military, industrial, and civilian mobilization."[40]

The National Security Council (NSC) that the NSA established has had lasting importance for presidential decision making. As designed in 1947, it was presided over by the president himself and included the vice-president, secretaries of state, defense, and the three military departments, as well as the chairman of the NSRB. The CIA reported to the NSC,

---

39   Trask, *DOD*, p. 9.

40   Bork, *Department*, pp. 40–41. Trask, *DOD*, p. 9. Cray, in *General*, p. 683, notes that Marshall, who was secretary of state at the time, only played a minor role in the passage of the National Security Act. See Condit, *Test*, p. 14, for more about NSRB.

and the director usually attended its meetings. The NSC had a wide-ranging remit to "advise the President with respect to the integration of domestic, foreign, and military policies relating to the national security so as to enable the military services and the other departments and agencies of the Government to cooperate more effectively in matters involving the national security." With four secretaries speaking for defense, it was difficult to make coherent decisions relating to military threats or needs.[41]

A further innovation of the NSA was formal creation of the Joint Chiefs of Staff (JCS). This had existed de facto since 1942, thanks to the urgency of war and the compatible personal chemistry of Admiral William D. Leahy, General George C. Marshall, Admiral Ernest J. King, and General Hap Arnold. But this wartime foursome had no statutory authority. In Marshall's words, they "went through the war period, you might say, with an 'unwritten constitution.'"[42] As Samuel P. Huntington described it, the JCS never had any firmer legal basis than an exchange of letters between Marshall and Admiral King.

Given the wartime exigencies, the services generally got what they wanted. To achieve ultimate victory, Congress was willing to "trust in God and General Marshall." Marshall "virtually dictated the budgets." The 1947 NSA made them a committee of equals and the "principal military advisers to the President and the Secretary of Defense." Not until 1949 was the position of Chairman of the JCS created.[43]

---

41   Trask, *DOD*, pp. 8-9. See Condit, *Test*, pp. 14 and 29 on how the NSC works.

42   "Prepare for 10 Years of Tension: An Interview with George C. Marshall," *U.S. News & World Report*, April 13, 1951, p. 27.

43   Huntington, *Soldier*, pp. 319, 325. Trask, *DOD*, p. 9. "Inside Story of Joint Chiefs of Staff," *U.S. News & World Report*, May 18, 1951, pp. 13–14.

SECRETARY JAMES V. FORRESTAL

George C. Marshall was only the third secretary of defense. The first was sworn in on September 17, 1947: James V. Forrestal. He was an investment banker who had received flight training with the Navy during the First World War. In August 1940, President Franklin D. Roosevelt appointed him undersecretary of the Navy. There he established a reputation as an efficient organizer and manager of the Navy's industrial mobilization and procurement. On May 19, 1944, he succeeded Frank Knox as Navy secretary when the latter suffered a fatal heart attack. Forrestal led the Navy through the closing year of the war and two years of painful demobilization. Thus he was a man well qualified for the new job. He was actively involved in devising and enacting the National Security Act and the new NME although he had been a vocal opponent of the unification of the forces.

Forrestal worked himself to mental exhaustion trying to make the new defense establishment work. He sought to obtain cooperation and action by seeking the mutual consent of all the key players, including the service secretaries and chiefs of staff. Instead, he experienced bitter battles among those players. The cause was usually the budget, which was never large enough to satisfy the services and secretaries. Debates seemed endless. Forrestal could not persuade the services that only by working together would they get most of what they needed. They blamed him for their problems and circumvented him and his office by going directly to Congress, as the 1947 NSA permitted them to do. He was unable to exercise the necessary "authority, direction, and control" because his power was only "general."[44]

Forrestal learned that the central weakness in the organization was the secretary of defense's lack of power in the face of three largely autonomous service secretaries. In the context of a

---

44   Kintner, *Forging*, pp. 26–27. Borklund, *Department*, pp. 49, 120.

constantly escalating Cold War, he was also convinced that America's defense spending had to increase. But he faced a president who was adamant about bringing the budget into balance after a long war and who therefore rejected the increase in funds the secretary of defense and the military wanted.

Forrestal ultimately concluded that the NSA did not function as it should. In his first report as secretary in December 1948, he noted that "the mere passage of the National Security Act did not mean the accomplishment of the objectives overnight. The most difficult part of the task of unification is to bring conflicting ideas into harmony." He became a convinced proponent of more complete unification. He made specific recommendations that ultimately resulted in a major amendment of the NSA in 1949.[45] President Truman picked up on Forrestal's proposals to improve the nation's defense structure. He forwarded the resulting changes to Congress on March 5, 1949.

The amendments were approved by Congress on August 10, 1949. At their core was the strengthening of the secretary of defense. The modifying word "general" was dropped from the "direction, authority, and control" he could exercise. The term, National Military Establishment, was scrapped and replaced by a full-fledged Department of Defense, and it became the only executive department in the realm of defense. The three service departments lost their cabinet status and were downgraded from executive to military departments. Their seats in the National Security Council were taken away. Only the secretary of defense would represent the defense establishment on the NSC. The service departments lost their right to go over the secretary of defense's head and appeal directly to the president or the Bureau of the Budget. The three joint chiefs and the service secretaries did retain their right, after informing the secretary of defense, to direct recommendations to Congress.

---

45   Trask, *DOD*, pp. 58–60. Borklund, *Department*, pp. 54–56.

In order to enable the strengthened secretary of defense to do his job more effectively, the amended National Security Act provided him with a deputy secretary of defense, a post that Marshall filled with Robert Lovett. It also allowed for three assistant secretaries of defense to perform any tasks the secretary prescribes.

Marshall later appointed Anna Rosenberg as Assistant Secretary of Defense for Manpower. Born in 1901 in Hungary of Jewish parents before moving as a child to New York City, she was a liberal and a fervent New Dealer. She had impressive experience. Presidents Roosevelt and Truman had sent her to Europe in 1944 and 1945 to get a better understanding of the Army's manpower problems. There she won the friendship of such top generals as Dwight D. Eisenhower and Walter Bedell Smith. She was one of the few who endorsed the concept of Universal Military Training. This was an idea that Marshall consistently advocated, but it was never popular in Congress and the public. Marshall's personal aide, Marshall Carter, remembered that "she was a great mediator. She had the happy faculty of understanding a problem before the people had expounded on what it was, and zeroed in on solutions. Most everybody who worked for her thought she walked on water." She was the first woman ever to have such a high post in the field of defense. She also had the honor of being the only official in the defense department whom Marshall addressed by her first name.[46]

To prevent the secretary of defense from enlarging his powers too much, certain limitations were imposed upon him. He was forbidden from transferring or consolidating any combat functions. Sensitive examples of this would be dissolving the Marines, as some Army supporters wanted, or combining naval aviation with the Air Force. Any noncombat functions that the secretary might want to transfer had to be reported to

---

46   Pogue, *Marshall*, pp. 430–31. Carter quote in Cray, *General*, p. 688.

Congress.[47] Nevertheless, the secretary of defense emerged from the amended NSA as the principal assistant to the president in matters of national defense, with control of the budget and funds.

JOINT CHIEFS OF STAFF

A new position of Chairman of the Joint Chiefs of Staff was created. He handles procedure, sets the agenda and selects the issues that would be discussed in the thrice weekly meetings in a well-guarded JCS conference room in the Pentagon. He operated under the specific limitation that he would not "exercise command." He would also have no vote in JCS decisions. The latter restriction proved irrelevant since the JCS never voted. The JCS reaches unanimous decisions. This was a carry-over from the Second World War. Marshall confirmed in an interview in *U.S. News & World Report* that within that earlier JCS, "We didn't vote on decisions. We avoided voting."[48]

During Marshall's tenure as secretary of defense, the country possessed a Joint Chiefs of Staff uniquely experienced as successful commanders during the Second World War: General J. Lawton "Lightning Joe" Collins, Army Chief of Staff; General Hoyt S. Vandenberg, Air Force Chief of Staff; and Admiral Forrest P. Sherman, Chief of Naval Operations. The Chairman of the Joint Chiefs of Staff was General Omar Bradley. Despite the trust in them that Marshall and President Truman had, they operated under definite limitations after the NSA was amended in 1949.

First, they had no direct access to the president. Any recommendations they wanted to pass on to the president had

---

47   Kintner, *Forging*, pp. 35–37.

48   "10 Years of Tension," *U.S. News*, p. 27. "Joint Chiefs of Staff," *U.S. News*, pp. 13–14. Note that NATO, which Marshall was helping to create, also never votes but decides by consensus.

to be in written form and be cleared by the secretary of defense. Normally they advised the defense secretary, who in turn discussed policy with the president. This did not mean that they never dealt with the president. The commander-in-chief could invite the Chairman of the Joint Chiefs or the three members for advice. General Omar Bradley, the chairman, met with Truman about twice a week. But he was invited to the White House to brief the president on military matters, not to transmit JCS decisions. In an interview with *U.S. News & World Report*, Marshall called the JCS "the strategy-planning body," a "very sound source of military advice." Its advice is directed mainly to the president, but also to the secretary of defense and the NSC. They never made a public appearance with him as secretary.[49]

Two examples demonstrate the defense secretary's role of directing advice coming from the JCS. In March 1951, the JCS advised that the issues of Communist China's entry into the UN and Peking's control of Formosa be excluded from any cease-fire terms in Korea. However, Marshall did not object to these matters being included in subsequent peace negotiations. Also when General Douglas MacArthur was dismissed from command on April 11, 1951, the JCS was asked for an opinion. Marshall met with them on April 8 to learn that they concurred unanimously with the president's decision to fire the general. But the JCS had no opportunity to present their views directly to the president.

The JCS has no direct contact with the National Security Council, where basic policy is discussed. They can present their views indirectly through the secretary of defense, who is the only person from the military side to have a seat in this body. President Truman did not regard the NSC as a body where decisions were made, but as an advisory organ. He often did not attend the meetings.

---

49   "10 Years of Tension," *U.S. News*, p. 27.

The JCS had no direct command over American fighting forces. Orders, directives, and reports had to be channeled through one of the three military services assigned to take the lead over a specific theater of operation. For example, during the Korean War, it was the Chief of the Army, General J. Lawton Collins, who issued orders to the UN commander there and to whom US commanders in Korea reported. They did not report directly to the JCS.[50]

SECRETARY LOUIS A. JOHNSON

The embattled Forrestal lost support of the budget-cutting President Truman, who grew tired of the defense secretary's continuing complaints that the defense budget was too small. He was asked to resign, and he left office on March 28, 1949, a broken and deeply depressed man. He suffered a mental breakdown and was sent to Bethesda Naval Medical Center. Two months later, on May 22, 1949, he committed suicide by leaping out of a sixth floor window. There is little doubt that the pressures of his eighteen-month tenure as defense secretary and his conviction that he had failed were largely responsible for this tragic act.[51]

He was replaced as secretary of defense in May 1949 by Louis A. Johnson, a graduate of University of Virginia Law School who practiced law in Clarksburg, West Virginia. He had long-standing ties with the military starting with his service as an Army officer in France during the First World War. He was a co-founder of the American Legion and was its national commander from 1932 to 1933. From 1937 to 1940, he was assistant secretary of war, during which time he advocated Marshall's pet project, Universal Military Training. He was a long-standing friend of President

---

50   "Joint Chiefs of Staff," *U.S. News,* pp. 13–14. Pogue, *Marshall,* pp. 438–40.

51   Trask, *DOD,* pp. 57–60. Borklund, *Department,* pp. 119–20.

Truman. What opened the door to his appointment as secretary of defense was his service as Truman's chief fund-raiser for the president's unexpected electoral victory in 1948. He supported the president's aims to control defense costs and to bring about the unification of the armed services.[52]

Johnson was a strapping strong-willed ambitious man whose determination facilitated the shift toward increased central control over department of defense by the secretary of defense. But he soon collided with the JCS and service secretaries because of what some would call ruthless decision making, arrogance, and failure to listen to advice from the services. The Navy was incensed by his lone decision to cancel further work on the $188 million super-carrier *United States* in April 1949, shortly after assuming office. This helped spark what became known as the "Revolt of the Admirals." They asked in despair what a flamboyant abrasive West Virginia lawyer, who was probably using the defense department as a stepping stone to the presidency, could possibly know about warships.

Naval officials responded by questioning publicly and in Congress the wisdom of acquiring the Air Force's strategic bomber, the B-36, thereby stoking animosity between the Navy and Air Force. The resulting infighting poisoned his relations with the services, devastated morale within the defense department, and weakened his standing with the president. When the Korean War broke out on June 25, 1950, many in Washington blamed him for the deplorable state in which the US military found itself.[53]

What made his dismissal unavoidable were his bitter differences with Secretary of State Dean Acheson and the

---

52   Truman was determined to spend no more than $11 billion on defense. Bork, *DOD*, p. 121.

53   Kintner, *Forging*, p. 47. Trask, *DOD*, pp. 61–63, Borklund, *Department*, p. 121. Condit, *Test*, p. 15.

disastrous performance of American military forces in the early months of the Korean War. The two secretaries not only had a deep personal aversion to each other, but they had serious policy disagreements. Johnson regarded Asia as the most important arena for American foreign policy. He avidly promoted support for non-Communist governments like the Nationalist Chinese regime on the island of Formosa. By stark contrast, Acheson believed that the primary battleground for US security was Europe. His opinion was supported by both the president and Marshall. Acheson and Johnson were on opposite sides of the debate in March 1950 that culminated in NSC 68, which, as we shall see later, called for a more rigorous containment of the Soviet Union. When the Truman administration got its first inkling that General Douglas MacArthur did not wholly agree with its policies, the State Department pressed for the general's dismissal, whereas Johnson adamantly rejected such a controversial move.[54]

Acheson exclaimed in despair that Johnson was "too outrageous to be explained by mere cussedness" and must have a brain malady; indeed he did die later of an illness of the brain. Acheson wrote in his memoirs that "Johnson's behavior had passed beyond the peculiar to the impossible." This hostility toward the secretary of state went so far as to restrict the working contacts between the two major departments. One of the first things Marshall did after assuming the office of secretary of defense was to restore these ties. But Johnson's dislike for Acheson became so strong that he hatched plans behind the president's back to have Acheson removed from office.[55]

---

54 Borklund, *Men of Pentagon*, p. 100. The *Sunday Oregonian* headline on September 17, 1950, read: "'Europe First' Expected Policy under Marshall." Marshall Library, Scrapbook box 214. For NSC 68, see later text in this chapter and Cray, *General*, p. 689.

55 Acheson quote in Condit, *Test*, p. 15. Acheson, *Present*, p. 441.

The crisis reached a boiling point in September 1950. The president had had enough of Johnson's rumored dabbling in presidential aspirations of his own and sabotaging the work of Secretary of State Acheson. He had already decided Johnson would have to go, but he was awaiting the right moment. A frustrated president charged that Johnson had an "inordinate egotistical desire to run the whole government" and succeeded in offending every single member of the cabinet.

The last straw came in a meeting Johnson had in his Pentagon office with Averell Harriman, who had just returned in late June 1950 from his assignment in Paris to help administer the Marshall plan. Johnson took a phone call from Senator Robert Taft of Ohio, a leading Republican who harbored his own ambitions to become president one day. Harriman listened while Johnson congratulated Taft for a rousing speech criticizing the secretary of state and called for Acheson's dismissal. After hanging up, Johnson turned to the president's trusted adviser and proposed that if Acheson could be sacked, then he would see to it that Harriman would become secretary of state. As soon as Harriman left the Pentagon, he reported to the president Johnson's surprising conversation with an opposition leader and his offer to Harriman. Truman found this story "almost incredible," even though it was conveyed by a man with a reputation for "absolute truth."[56]

Truman had already decided before the outbreak of the Korean War that Johnson was a liability and would have to be dismissed. After returning from his Michigan vacation, Marshall met with Truman in the Blair House on September 6 and was asked to become secretary of defense to help the country out of its current crisis in Asia. Almost seventy years old with a serious kidney operation behind him, from which he never fully recovered, Marshall was not as vigorous as he had once been.

---

56   Condit, *Test*, p. 33.

The normally serious ex-general joked about the intense concern about his health. He asked why the photographers were taking so many pictures of him at Red Cross headquarters, "except to prove that I'm not dead yet."[57]

As we have seen, Marshall agreed to serve for six months to a year if Robert Lovett could be his deputy and take over when Marshall had to leave. It is certain that the general was not swayed by personal financial arguments. Congress had allowed him to keep his commission and his annual Army retirement pay of $18,761. This was topped off with $3,739 pay for serving as secretary of defense. The grand total of $22,500 was the salary of a cabinet officer at the time.[58] With Marshall's acceptance in his pocket, President Truman met with Johnson on September 11 and demanded his resignation. The outgoing secretary of defense saw his presidential hopes go up in smoke, and he was speechless. He left office September 19, 1950.

The department of defense came under new management on September 21, and the Pentagon rejoiced, as did many in the media and public. *The New York Times* described the new secretary of defense as "a man of great force, immense experience, and keen foresight, to whom no aura of politics attaches and in whom the people place unbounded confidence." It predicted that Marshall would put an end to the battles going on between State and Defense and among the services. The *Washington Post* praised Marshall as a military man with a civilian mind, a "truly authentic American in his respect for and devotion to our American system of government." There were some anti-Truman newspapers, such as the *Chicago Tribune*, which dug up some of the old accusations that Marshall had lost China and left Korea defenseless. Marshall had reminded Truman that such mud would be flung again, but the president chose to disregard

---

57   *Chicago Sun-Times,* September 17, 1950.

58   Condit, *Test,* p. 35.

it and to look forward to coping with the daunting challenges that faced the country.[59]

NSC 68

Shortly before the onset of the Korean War in June 1950, an elite study group produced a document that greatly influenced the way the Truman administration and Marshall viewed what seemed to be an increasingly menacing world: NSC 68. The key figure in producing this important document was Paul H. Nitze, successor to George Kennan as director of the State Department's Policy Planning Staff. The group he chaired was concerned that the Cold War had become more threatening to the US and its allies. This worry became especially urgent in September 1949, when the Soviet Union successfully tested its first atom bomb. It perceived that the Soviet threat was not only military, but also ideological, global, and total. The Soviet Union's leaders were determined to maintain absolute power in all the regions they controlled, to extend their domination over the Eurasian land mass, to eliminate all opposition to their rule, and to subvert or destroy the United States, their principal enemy. The drafters did not argue that the Soviets had in mind "deliberate armed action involving the United States at this time." But the document pointed to the possibility of war through misinterpretation or miscalculation.

This influential study predicted a further deterioration in the world situation. It spoke of the need to contain Soviet communism "by all means short of war," including forcing its leaders to obey generally accepted standards of international behavior. The report emphasized that the US must build up its

---

59 Condit, *Test*, pp. 33–34. Pogue, *Marshall*, pp. 422–23. For press reaction to Marshall's appointment, see Marshall Library Scrapbook boxes 214–17. For Marshall's confirmation in the Senate, see Unger, *Marshall*, p. 460.

and its allies' military strength while it had its powerful atomic deterrent and try to reduce Moscow's power and influence in perimeter areas. It should encourage the independence of Soviet satellites.[60]

The service secretaries and the JCS endorsed this study even before it reached Louis Johnson's desk. At first, he objected to the report. Nevertheless, he signed it and submitted it to the president on April 7, 1950. Truman in turn submitted it to the National Security Council (NSC) five days later. Both the president and Defense Secretary Johnson were among those who had serious qualms about the document. It called for a major buildup of America's and its allies' military strength. The US was relatively new on the world stage. But by the time the Korean War broke out on June 25, 1950, it had shown toughness in Iran in 1946, Turkey and Greece in 1947, the Middle East in 1948, and Germany, especially the Berlin Airlift in 1948 and 1949. In June 1950, it faced a powerful and initially successful North Korean attack against what would later become an American ally: South Korea. By taking up the fight in Korea and dramatically raising the nation's defense budgets, the Truman government made the report a reality and transformed the ideas behind NSC 68 into policy. America's global role grew.

NSC 68 flew in the face of Johnson's and Truman's determination to keep military expenditures low. But Pyongyang's invasion made their position impossible. The president approved NSC 68 in late 1950–early 1951. Congress did not formally approve it in 1950, and it remained a classified document for twenty-five years.

Consensus grew in the nation's capital that the North Korean attack demonstrated that the Soviet Union might indeed be prepared to unleash overt military aggression outside Eastern Europe. Johnson himself had warned that North Korea's attack

---

60 Condit, *Test*, pp. 6–7.

risked "starting a third world war." It would be up to the country's third secretary of defense, George C. Marshall, to meet this first great challenge to an infant untried department of defense that had existed only three years and had borne that name only a year and a half. It increased in size because of the war in Korea. But it grew in power and stature because of the leadership Marshall provided in his one year in office. His duties involved restoring and strengthening military preparedness, elaborating global strategy and policy, maintaining civilian control over the military in a democratic country, preserving the inseparability of military from political questions, and gaining the respect and support of foreign allies. These were all problems Marshall had mastered before.[61]

---

61   Condit, *Test,* pp. 6–11, 39. Stoler, *Marshall,* pp. 177, 180–81. On September 18, 1950, the *Phoenix Republic* published the headline: "Trusted Pilot at the Helm."

CHAPTER TWO

A New Style of Leadership in the Pentagon

MARSHALL IMMEDIATELY SET ABOUT TO RESTORE THE BADLY SHAKEN morale in the Pentagon and to mend the severed ties with the department of state. Overnight the new department's relations with the nation's diplomats improved dramatically. The first and most public evidence was seen in the deference Marshall rendered to his former assistant at the state department, Secretary of State Dean Acheson. Referring to Marshall's appointment, Acheson later admitted that "no change could have been more welcome to me." But he confessed to a certain embarrassment. Recognizing that the state department outranked the defense department in protocol and that the secretary of state was the senior cabinet officer, Marshall never went through a door before Acheson or walked anywhere but to his left. Acheson remembered that Marshall would go around an automobile to get in after Acheson and to sit on the left side. In meetings, Marshall never spoke before the secretary of state and always sat on the same side of the table as Acheson. He waived off all protests on Acheson's part.

"To be treated so by a revered and beloved former chief was a harrowing experience, but the result in government was, I think, unique in the history of the Republic. For the first time and,

Marshall with Secretary of State Dean Acheson.

perhaps,...the last, the Secretaries of State and Defense, with their top advisers, met with the Chiefs of Staff in their map room and discussed common problems together." Those meetings took place on a regular basis, and their staffs and mid- and lower-level personnel, the people Marshall called "the pick-and-shovel men," also enjoyed routine contact with each other.

Officials from the CIA were invited to JCS meetings. Acheson went on to tell of an agreement he made with General Omar Bradley: that "the phrases 'from a military point of view' and 'from a political point of view' were excluded from our talks. No such dichotomy existed. Each of us had our tactical and strategic problems, but they were interconnected, not separate." Acheson wrote that this agreement was "scrupulously observed."[1]

---

1   Numerous documents in the Marshall Library's archives indicate that the phrase "from the military point of view" did indeed continue to appear in some memos and other communications. A cartoon in the *Sunday Oregonian* on September 17, 1950, showed phone lines down between the Pentagon and State Department and Marshall as a lineman coming to fix it.

On Marshall's watch the nation's strategy included both political and military considerations. Foreign and defense policy were parts of a whole again. This did not mean that the department of defense actually made policy. In an April 13, 1951, interview with *U.S. News & World Report*, Marshall responded to a question whether his department initiates foreign policy by saying: "No. We execute it so far as it involves matters of a military nature, and we bring our influence to bear when the foreign policy proposed has military implications."[2]

Samuel Huntington argued in *The Soldier and the State* that Marshall as secretary of defense came closest to functioning purely as a military spokesman." He explained that this was indicated by the "essentially passive concept he had of his duties," not attempting to be an initiator of or contributor to policy. This was a critique of Marshall since Huntington's opinion was that the secretary of defense should be a man of policy. One of Marshall's aides expressed the issue this way: "It points up to the military the political implications of what they do."[3] Marshall later told his biographer, Forrest C. Pogue, that there had been an ongoing battle between the Air Force and the Navy and later between the military services and the State Department. "I healed them all up in about two weeks and it never got to the press."[4]

The highest military officers in the Pentagon, who had been embittered by Johnson, were soldiers with whom Marshall had had long and close association. They regarded each other with great mutual respect. This was a critical ingredient in Marshall's influence within the Pentagon. A successful secretary is dependent

---

2   "10 Years of Tension," *U.S. News*, p. 30.

3   Huntington, *Soldier*, pp. 442, 453–55. Acheson, *Present*, p. 441. Pogue, *Marshall*, p. 437. Borklund, *Men of Pentagon*, p. 102.

4   Larry Bland, ed. *George C. Marshall: Interviews and Reminiscences for Forrest C. Pogue*, p. 311.

upon an effective and cooperative JCS. These included General Omar Bradley, Chairman of the JCS. He had known Marshall since he was an instructor at Fort Benning in the late 1920s. He had been one of the key commanders in Europe during the Second World War and was recognized as a "Marshall man." Although they were occasionally hunting buddies, Bradley never called Marshall anything but "General Marshall." Even though he knew that Marshall had instructed all officers simply to enter his DOD office immediately when there were issues to be dealt with, Bradley always asked the assistant if it were OK for him to enter the room. The two men worked very well together. Bradley was also well-liked by President Truman, a fellow Missourian. This kind of support was needed to strengthen a position that was new and undeveloped. [5]

Army Chief of Staff, J. Lawton Collins, was also a favored "Marshall man." They had been friends since their Fort Benning days in the 1920s, and he had assigned Collins the important task to work up a plan for reorganizing the Army's divisions. He had commanded one of the two corps that hit the beaches in Normandy. His daring earned him the name of "Lightnin' Joe" and made him an obvious choice to fill Bradley's former position as Army Chief of Staff. In the ongoing war in Korea, he was the JCS member who oversaw the military side of the war effort.[6]

Air Force Chief of Staff General Hoyt Vandenberg, nephew of Senator Arthur Vandenberg, was not as familiar to the new secretary of defense as were Bradley and Collins. But he had held many top positions in the Army Air Corps and had led Central Intelligence after the war, the predecessor organization to the CIA, before becoming Chief of the Air Force. Chief of Naval Operations Admiral Forrest Sherman was also not an intimate of Marshall. But the secretary respected his outstanding

---

5   Pogue, *Marshall,* pp. 438–39.

6   Pogue, *Marshall,* pp. 439–40.

*Generals Dwight D. Eisenhower and George C. Marshall in Algiers,
1943. Note that one officer has his stars on the wrong collar.*

performance in the Pacific as Admiral Chester W. Nimitz's
Chief of Plans in the Pacific.

Understandably Marshall was very close to Dwight D.
Eisenhower, who left the presidency of Columbia University
to become NATO's first Supreme Allied Commander in
Europe (SACEUR) in 1951. Other military officers who played
important roles in the Korean conflict, such as Generals Matthew
Ridgeway and James Van Fleet, had been victorious commanders
in Europe who had reached high command because they had
been recorded positively in Marshall's imaginary "black book."
President Truman was largely guided in his appointments by
the desire to utilize the popularity of these top Second World
War commanders. During the Second World War, Marshall
had reportedly confused Van Fleet with a less talented officer

he had once observed. Realizing his mistake, he promoted Van Fleet quickly through the ranks. Marshall was famous for his great memory, but he was reportedly bad at remembering the names of his staff.[7]

Marshall's behavior and individual style differed dramatically from that of his aggressive acerbic predecessor. Louis Johnson was always suspicious that people in the state department, like Averell Harriman, were trying to get his job. In social situations, the new secretary was friendly and warm and willing to have one drink with other guests. He was considerate, and he remembered to direct small kindnesses to the families of his subordinates or commanders. He could almost be grandfatherly. His correspondence was voluminous.

He was known by intimates to have had a dry wit. He provided an example when he learned that Vernon A. Walters had been promoted to the temporary grade of lieutenant colonel on November 3, 1950. Marshall wrote to Averell Harriman that "the old army custom is to drop the new insignia in a glass of hard liquor, drink the liquor, and then fasten the insignia on the tunic. As Walters is a teetotaler, it looks like you will have to use milk or water!"[8]

Marshall's nickname among his step-children was "Colonel." His fellow VMI cadets referred to him as "Pug." On the job he was rather aloof, and some persons, including some foreign leaders like General Sir Alan Brooke and the postwar British foreign secretary, Ernest Bevin, found him forbidding. He maintained a certain distance with everybody, including close associates. Except for Anna Rosenberg and former Second World War aide Frank McCarthy, he addressed his colleagues and subordinates by last names only. For example, letters to

7   Pogue, *Marshall*, pp. 439–40. Huntington, *Soldier*, p. 359. Borklund, *Men of Pentagon*, p. 103.

8   Marshall Library, folder 2, 2606, Box 577.

General Eisenhower were addressed, "Dear Eisenhower." Only once did he slip and call him "Ike" when they were both being honored by a ticker-tape parade in New York City. The victorious commander had just returned from the European battlefield in 1945. An embarrassed Marshall immediately realized his mistake and corrected himself. However, his admiration for Eisenhower could not be denied. On V-E Day (May 8, 1945) he sent the triumphant Allied commander a glowing tribute: "You have completed your mission with the greatest victory in the history of warfare. You have commanded with outstanding success the most powerful military force that has ever been assembled...you have made history, great history for the good of mankind."[9]

Everybody, including the president himself and Secretary of State Acheson, referred to him as "General Marshall," and he invariably answered the telephone, "General Marshall speaking." In order not to distract others, he seldom wandered the halls of the Pentagon, and he had precious few drop-in visitors to his office. He had fewer front people and aides outside his office than some of his subordinates. They were instructed simply to enter the room without a salute or fanfare, sit down and get right to work.

Like General Eisenhower, he had learned in his long career to control his temper although his wife, Katherine, wrote in her 1946 book about her life as an Army wife that he could explode at home against others on the job.[10] Nobody ever got a tongue-lashing, and very seldom did he raise his voice. Those who expressed an opinion he found unreasonable might notice his icy demeanor or hear a reply from him like "please repeat

---

9   Robert H. Ferrell, ed., *Off the Record: The Private Papers of Harry S. Truman*, p. 214. *Marshall Papers*, Vol. 7, documents 316, 324. Marshall quote in William I. Hitchcock, *The Age of Eisenhower: America and the World in the 1950s*, p. 25.

10   Pogue, *Marshall*, p. 496.

what you were saying." Those who did not measure up were usually not peremptorily dismissed. But the general might say to his subordinates something like: "Hasn't so-and-so indicated a desire to serve in North Africa for a while?" The person would disappear to another assignment. Seldom would he be as blunt as he once was during the Second World War. A subordinate officer who had gotten orders to leave for Europe the next day told him that he could not depart since his wife was out of town and no provisions had been made to move their furniture. He noticed the stony look on Marshall's face. "Oh, I'm sorry," the officer said, to which the general replied: "So am I. You'll be retiring tomorrow."

All agreed that he inspired respect, even awe. Dean Acheson remembered his presence in the state department, which was a "striking and communicative force. His figure conveyed intensity, which his voice, low, staccato, and incisive, reinforced. It compelled respect. It spread a sense of authority and of calm. There was no military glamour about him and nothing of the martinet." He was aware that his modesty could inspire good performance by his peers and subordinates. He was once quoted as saying: "There is no limit to the good one can do if he doesn't care who gets the credit." He applied that insight throughout his career as general and public servant. His long-time executive, Marshall S. Carter, remembered that "he was intensely practical, oriented to getting things done...things just started to happen, he made things go."[11]

Marshall's energizing the department of defense was not all that he contributed. As he had done at the state department almost three years earlier, he applied his talent for rationalizing and organizing the policymaking process. When he had shown up at the state department in January 1947, he was appalled by the organization he found. There were nineteen independent

11   Condit, *Test*, pp. 35–36.

officials who reported directly to the secretary of state. Working-level cooperation was undeveloped, rudimentary, and sometimes consciously avoided altogether.

Applying his military experience, he established an executive secretariat of bright young foreign service officers who stopped each request heading for Marshall's desk and rerouted it to all the bureaus that had some interest or authority in the matter. If it could be solved below the level of secretary, then the responsible leaders should do it. This was the civilian application of what he had always said to his military subordinates during the Second World War: Don't debate a problem, solve it!

Thus by the time Marshall actually saw a paper, it had already been commented on by all the offices concerned. This way, what reached his eyes had been examined and considered and cross-referenced by all major players. He seldom had to make a decision on a subject more than once. He was most renowned for his decision making. He made them quickly and with assurance. He never brooded over a decision he had made. He believed that such brooding would never improve a decision, and a leader had to move on. One state department assistant described the resulting process so: "The 'Old Man' was a great one for orderly conduct of business and for those people who had responsibility getting their day in court before a decision was reached." His subordinates were aware of Marshall's dislike of intrigue and of his insistence on loyalty and responsibility up and down a clear chain of command.[12]

A noticeable personal practice he demonstrated to the department of defense's personnel was to protect their health. He worked much shorter hours than his predecessors, arriving in his office at 7:30 a.m. and leaving normally by about 4:30 p.m. This was not solely because he was seventy years old and was not in his peak of health. He had experienced several breakdowns

---

12   Borklund, *Men of Pentagon*, p. 94.

during his earlier Army years caused by overwork and fatigue. He had also seen the country's first secretary of defense, James Forrestal, literally work himself to death. Thus he did not take much work home and encouraged others in the Pentagon to do the same. He explained this: "There is only so much productive work in a man. There comes a time in the day when your efforts no longer have any meaning. Your energy is gone. When you pass that point, you are operating on reflexes. The loss then is that of whatever faculties make you better than run-of-the-mill. So, when you go home, relax." He believed that the limit to a man's productivity is reached at 3:00 p.m.[13]

He was ever the pragmatist. During his time in service, he saw that certain matters that came into the Pentagon on Friday could not await a decision on Monday. Therefore he agreed that important staff personnel had to be at work Saturday mornings to deal with such urgent issues. When the work load was especially heavy, the work week could be raised to forty-eight hours.

Marshall quickly reorganized the peak of the Pentagon staff to work in the same way. He thereby created in a time of crisis a symbol of stability, enhanced by his own reputation as the organizer of past military victory. He was respected, even beloved, by most Americans. Thanks to his successful Marshall Plan, he enjoyed the support and sympathy of America's allies in the UN and NATO. This was essential given the frightening challenges his nation faced.

MARSHALL PICKS HIS TEAM

The amended National Security Act of 1949 created new top positions in the department of defense in order to enable the secretary to manage the ever-growing and already largest part of the federal government with more than 2,700 employees,

---

13 Borklund, *Men of Pentagon*, pp. 111–12. *Marshall Papers*, Vol. 7, document 196.

mostly civilians. Marshall appointed the first deputy secretary of defense, Robert A. Lovett, who succeeded Marshall as secretary in September 1951 and remained in office until January 20, 1953. The secretary was also granted three assistant secretary positions, whose responsibilities he as secretary could define. To deal with the all-important subject of manpower, including his pet project, Universal Military Training, he created the first post focusing on manpower. He appointed the first woman, Anna M. Rosenberg, to hold such a high post in the department. He retained Marx Leva as his assistant secretary for legal and legislative affairs and Wilfred J. McNeil as comptroller.[14]

His chief executive officer, some would say his "right-hand man," was Colonel Marshall S. Carter. He rose to the rank of Lieutenant General and after retirement served as president of the George C. Marshall Research Foundation in Lexington, Virginia. Carter expressed his esteem for his boss in a July 1972 *Reader's Digest* article. He described as "awesome" the secretary's "imperturbability under pressure," and he was struck by Marshall's "no-nonsense approach to the crushing demands." Carter did not deny the fact that Marshall had an "austere presence" and that his "icy manner, the frightening, cold-blue eyes" could be intimidating. But behind this stiff exterior was "a warm and quietly humorous human being" who "loved a joke." Carter's loyalty toward him never wavered.[15]

The Marshall Foundation archives are full of communications from Carter to Marshall. They contain many memos and drafts of talking points and suggested texts directed to the secretary by Carter and others. In almost all cases, however, Marshall carefully read through them and made detailed substantive and

---

14   For the organization and reorganization of DOD, see *Marshall Papers,* Vol. 7, pp. 371–72 and documents 299, 445, and 451–52. See also documents 135, 151, and 183.

15   *Marshall Papers,* Vol. 7, document 352.

stylistic changes in his own hand. Marshall wrote all of his own speeches in longhand.[16]

Lovett was a man of enormous achievement, experience and intelligence. He had been a naval aviator in World War I who had become wealthy as an international banker in New York. He gained valuable defense experience while serving as assistant secretary of war for air under Henry L. Stimson from 1941 to 1945. He was a persuasive proponent of American air power and oversaw the massive expansion of the Army Air Force. He came back to Washington from 1947 to 1949 to be Marshall's under secretary of state during the latter's entire term of service as the nation's top diplomat. When Marshall accepted the president's request to become secretary of defense, he had made Lovett's appointment a condition, describing him to Truman as being "decisive, specific, frank." The two agreed on almost everything, including the military's role in government. Thanks in part to his gracious treatment of people, Lovett was able to persuade them gradually and willingly to accept his opinions. He preferred to convince through cooperation and was usually successful in keeping disagreements on a professional level.

One of Lovett's key assets was the total trust the president had for him. He was well liked within the department and was respected by the JCS. Lovett assumed the main burden of administration, doing whatever was necessary to lighten Marshall's work load. He maintained firm control on the organization. Many archival documents bear his signature over a broad range of issues, including the military buildup, NATO, and especially the budget. He agreed with Marshall that it had been a serious mistake to demobilize so quickly after World War II. "We did not just demobilize....We just disintegrated." But he shared with Marshall the view that military requirements should not override other governmental needs except in time of

---

16   Borklund, *Men of Pentagon*, pp. 90, 103. Condit, *Test*, pp. 35–36.

*Marshall and Assistant Secretary for
Manpower and Personnel Anna Rosenberg.*

crisis, such as the nation was facing at that time. He argued that
the objective was a good military "cruising speed," changing
to meet various contingencies. In Marshall's words, "Lovett
carries out the policies I have announced. He is in complete
charge of operations."[17]

The most daring appointment by far was Anna M. Rosenberg.
The new secretary considered the issues of manpower and
personnel to be of such cardinal importance that he elevated
the directorship over both of these fields to the level of assistant
secretary.[18] She was an unlikely defense department appointment
in that era, being a Jewish immigrant from Hungary, a New Yorker,

---

17   Condit, *Test*, pp. 35–39. Borklund, *Department*, p. 122. Trask, *DOD*,
      pp. 67–68.

18   Condit, *Test*, p. 35.

and especially a woman. Her qualifications were impeccable. Head of a public relations company since the 1920s, she was an avid New Dealer who had served on numerous public-service boards, including ones related to defense and war manpower. During the war years, she had served on the President's Labor Advisory Board and then on the Advisory Board of the Office of War Mobilization and Reconversion. Presidents Roosevelt and Truman sent her on missions to Europe in 1944 and 1945 to look into manpower difficulties. While there she struck up friendships with both General Eisenhower and General Walter Bedell Smith. She caught Marshall's eye as member of the Advisory Board on Universal Military Training, one of his most persistent pet projects. For her service she was awarded the Medal of Freedom and Medal of Merit.

Marshall gave her fair warning that if she accepted his offer of the assistant secretaryship, she would be viciously attacked by the same people who had taken him into their sights. She nevertheless accepted the job, but recommended that her appointment not be revealed until after the upcoming congressional elections. President Truman announced her recess appointment November 15, 1950. Her month-long confirmation process before the Senate Armed Services Committee proved as troublesome and personal as Marshall had predicted. This was the heyday of Senator Joseph McCarthy's anti-Communist hysteria, when Marshall in his own hearings had been called "a living lie" and "an errand boy, a front man, a stooge, or a conspirator for this Administration's crazy assortment of collectivist cutthroat crackpots and Communist fellow-travelling appeasers."[19]

Rosenberg fared no better, and she was sure that the attacks stemmed from her support of a national health insurance. Two congressmen announced that they were in possession of reliable

---

19   Jenner quote from Pogue, *Marshall*, pp. 426–27, Stoler, *Marshall*, pp. 182–83.

information that Anna Rosenberg was a Communist and an activist in Communist organizations. They said that FBI files backed up this charge. Not surprisingly these charges crumbled under close scrutiny. The man who had allegedly seen her several times at the John Reed Club recanted his story.

Rosenberg's many friends and admirers supported her ratification with telegrams and letters to the committee. They included Eisenhower, Walter Bedell Smith, who by then had become CIA director, and ex-Secretary of State James F. Byrnes, Marshall's predecessor as secretary of state. Eleanor Roosevelt asked her what she could do to help her. Marshall used his long-standing contacts with senators to press Rosenberg's case. He requested the FBI to show him the files it had on her, and they were made available to three of the committee members. They assured the whole committee that there was nothing in the files to substantiate the charges against her.

The FBI played a key role in removing the doubts about her. It found another Anna Rosenberg in California who had indeed been a member of the John Reed Club in New York before moving west. A grateful Marshall called and wrote to FBI director, J. Edgar Hoover, to thank him for removing the obstacles to her Senate approval. On December 14, the committee dismissed the outrageous charges against her and recommended her confirmation. A two-thirds majority of senators, including Joseph McCarthy, did this. Marshall was so nervous about the vote in the plenary that he instructed Mrs. Rosenberg to interrupt his meeting with the Joint Chiefs of Staff to inform him of the final vote. Choked up about the positive result, she did just that, bursting into the room to tell him. He replied: "That's good. Go home and get a facial; you look like hell." The gentlemen in uniform appeared shocked that the secretary would even know what a "facial" is.[20]

---

20   For the Rosenberg appointment, see Pogue, *Marshall*, pp. 430–36.

With his country in crisis and his team in place, Secretary of Defense Marshall turned his full attention to the fragile peace and inadequate defense in Europe and to the desperate fighting testing American and UN allied soldiers to the limit in Korea.

Quote is on p. 436. For Rosenberg, see *Marshall Papers*, Vol. 7, documents 135, 151, 183.

CHAPTER THREE

Marshall and the Defense of Europe

IN A LETTER TO WINSTON S. CHURCHILL, DATED JANUARY 3, 1951, George C. Marshall stated the obvious: "I was called back into service at a rather difficult time." The *Washington Post* headline on October 1, 1950, was no exaggeration: "Great Tasks Face General Marshall." Not only did he have to achieve unity at the Pentagon and with the State Department and the Western allies, but he had to work effectively and convincingly with Congress to fund a much larger military force. His country was involved in a bitter, difficult war in Korea, where the situation for American troops had been deteriorating by the day. Entire units had been surrounded and captured by battle-hardened and highly motivated Chinese Communist troops. He recalled in a speech given on May 21, 1951, that "the hostile invasion of Korea was probably the most critical test this country has ever faced."[1]

The war in Korea not only gave new life to the United Nations. It elevated the North Atlantic Treaty Organization (NATO) from being "only a paper promise" with "no teeth" and with partners who "were not absolutely certain as to the determination

---

1   *Marshall Papers*, Vol. 7, document 199.

of the United States" to a credible defense organization. As the father of the Marshall Plan, he enjoyed an indispensable advantage. To cite the *Milwaukee Journal* on November 12, 1950, he was considered to be a "towering world figure to the people of Europe...a soldier with a distaste for militarism."[2]

Marshall was deeply occupied in the effort to construct a credible defense of Europe against an overwhelmingly superior Soviet military in a region where America's primary security interests were at stake. In a letter dated October 11, 1950, one month after he assumed the office of secretary of defense, he wrote: "As you would anticipate, I am terribly busy now in connection with the North Atlantic Pact Meeting, of which I am the Chairman."[3]

His main challenge was to persuade Europeans, especially the French, that the only possible way of mounting a credible European defense was to permit West Germany to rearm. That was unthinkable for many Europeans after the brutal occupation regimes they had suffered so recently.[4] Cooperating in defense and creating an integrated Allied command in peacetime were bold leaps in themselves. But it took a lot to get used to having Germans as allies. German neutrality was appealing both in Germany and elsewhere in Europe.

The two separate commitments on opposite sides of the Earth were linked. The Korean War helped save NATO in that it prompted many allies to conclude that the war in Asia was a distraction and could be followed by a Soviet attack in Europe with forces that since 1949 were equipped with atomic weapons.[5] It persuaded many that the USSR was willing to use force even

2   *Marshall Papers,* Vol. 7, document 303.

3   *Marshall Papers,* Vol. 7, document 127.

4   Tony Judt, *Postwar: A History of Europe Since 1945,* p. 151.

5   Judt, *Postwar,* p. 151.

though Soviet troops were not actively involved. The ongoing Korean War made European allies more receptive to Marshall's arguments for a rearmed Germany and a more effective NATO alliance.

The very next day after being sworn in as secretary of defense, Marshall had to fly to New York to attend a meeting of "the big three" North Atlantic Treaty foreign and defense ministers: American, British, and French. Few public servants would have had the experience and factual knowledge to jump into such complicated and delicate talks with only a few hours to prepare. Marshall possessed an intimate knowledge of European political and military leaders, as well as of the struggling families who benefited from the Marshall Plan assistance.

MARSHALL'S PRIOR INVOLVEMENT WITH EUROPE

As a breveted full colonel in the First World War, Marshall had not only worked with Allied officers to draw up plans to move tens of thousands of Allied troops under the cover of darkness to other positions in the lines. As the aide to General John "Black Jack" Pershing, he was often in the presence of Europeans leaders. As General of the Army in the Second World War, he dealt with the allied nations' supreme military and political leadership. He became keenly aware of their desires, needs, limits, and fears. As a result of his wartime leadership and the admiration stemming from his postwar Marshall Plan, he enjoyed immense approval in the Allied publics and governing circles. The respect given him was an important asset in the negotiations to mount a feasible defense of Europe.

As secretary of state from January 1947 to January 1949, he experienced the collapse of Allied cooperation with the Soviet Union and the onset of the Cold War. The Foreign Ministers' Conference in Moscow failed in April 1947. Before departing Marshall had a frustrating meeting in the middle of the night with Stalin. He got the distinct impression that the Soviet leader was merely waiting for the Western European countries to collapse from extreme economic difficulties and fall into the Soviet Union's control. This was the defining moment for Marshall. The follow up meeting in Paris from June 27 to July 2, 1947, accomplished nothing. Therefore the US and the United Kingdom (UK) pressed forward with plans to meld their two zones of occupation in Germany and to bring about German economic recovery. No more concessions were sought by either side.

A frustrated President Truman declared in June 1946: "I'm tired of babying the Russians." On March 12, 1947, he had announced to Congress his Truman Doctrine: "It must be the policy of the United States to support free peoples who are resisting attempted subjugation by armed minorities or outside pressure."[6] Since an economically weakened Britain could no longer guarantee protection to Greece and Turkey, the US had to step in. Looking back on May 25, 1951, Marshall asserted that "we saved Greece from the communist overrunning, which means in effect we saved Italy and Turkey to a large extent." In his opinion, this policy also had contributed to Yugoslavia's break from Stalin in 1948.[7] Further poisoning the air between the former allies was the founding in October 1947 of the Cominform in Moscow. It replaced the earlier Comintern and was calculated to coordinate a communist propaganda offensive against the United States and its Western partners.

The sense that the Western allies and the West Germans had important common objectives was strengthened by the communist seizure of power in Czechoslovakia on February 20, 1948. The country had functioned since 1945 as a parliamentary democracy. This unexpected event advanced the military

---

6   Judt, *Postwar*, pp. 109, 124–27.

7   *Marshall Papers*, Vol. 7, document 309.

rethinking that had already been underway. Many saw the hand of Stalin at work, and war seemed much more likely. Few doubted that a Cold War had begun. In this tense and dangerous environment Congress rapidly approved the Marshall Plan.

Strengthening even further the sense that the Western allies and West Germany had common objectives was the Berlin Blockade from June 1948 to May 1949 following a currency reform in the West. The Soviets apparently expected that the Western allies could be forced to relinquish their rights in Berlin and to abandon the city. The American and British reaction was to organize an aerial supply line between the Western zones and the besieged city. Marshall had been able to convince doubting British leaders that the undertaking "was entirely practicable" and that the US was "going to do it whether they did or not. That was that." This seemingly impossible task, which even included transporting coal by air, sparked imagination and admiration. Several hundred American and British aircraft carried up to 12,000 tons of supplies to West Berlin each day. The operation's success, combined with the effect of adverse world opinion, forced the Soviets to lift the blockade.

This was the first time the Western allies signaled in no uncertain terms that they would resist the creeping Soviet takeover of the eastern part of Europe. For Germany it signaled a shift from being a defeated and distrusted enemy to being an inseparable friend and ally of the Western partners. On May 25, 1951, Marshall argued that it had been "a great victory psychologically and actually we didn't get into war doing it."[8]

American leaders became convinced that US policy should shed its punitive aspects and shift toward wholehearted support of the democratic potential in Europe, including Germany. In a letter to his wife, Mamie, NATO commander Eisenhower had expressed shock at the destruction visited on Germany.

---

8   *Marshall Papers*, Vol. 7, document 309.

"The country is devastated....Whole cities are obliterated. And the German population, to say nothing of millions of former slave laborers, is largely homeless....It is a bleak picture....In my wildest nightmares I never visualized some of the things now thrown at me." He was happy to leave the presidency of Columbia University and put on his uniform as NATO's SACEUR. In a letter to his friend, Swede Hazlett, he confessed that "I rather look on this effort as about the last remaining chance for the survival of western civilization."[9] Germany, not France, would be revived as the motor for European recovery. It would be Marshall's task to persuade the French government that partnership in defense must also include a democratic West Germany.

Nothing brought Marshall as much recognition and influence in post-war Europe as the European Recovery Program (ERP), which bore his name: the Marshall Plan. It was proposed in brief remarks he made at the Harvard University graduation on June 5, 1947. He pointed to the economic dislocation in Europe and the starvation that was near. The remedy for these problems was a renewal of Europeans' confidence in their economic future. It was in America's interest to tackle these problems because of its economic ties with Europe. Also there could be no assured peace or political stability without normal economic health. In addition, the kind of free institutions that the United States promotes in the world depended on the revival of working economies. European unity and cooperation were encouraged by the requirement that the Europeans themselves decide how the Marshall Plan money would be distributed and spent. Marshall traveled to France in November 1948, after a wave of left-wing strikes had largely collapsed, to see whether his plan was working. He determined that France was on the road to recovery.[10]

---

9   Hitchcock, *Eisenhower*, pp. 29, 49, 51.

10   Antony Beevor and Artemis Cooper, *Paris: After the Liberation, 1944–1947*, p. 369.

"Rubble Women" in Berlin. Entire families form a crew of builders working on a block of apartments funded by the Marshall Plan.

By the end of 1952, when Marshall Plan aid was terminated, the US had spent more than $13 billion, more than all earlier US foreign assistance combined. In the twenty-first century such a program would cost well over $100 billion. Aid was offered to the Soviet Union and its occupied countries, but Stalin was suspicious of American intentions and therefore forbade his country and its satellites from participating. This absence of communist countries as partners was fortuitous. It made it easier for Truman to get the ERP accepted by Congress.[11]

EUROPE FIRST

It became obvious very soon that Allied cooperation with the Soviet Union was impossible after the Second World War, given

---

11   Judt, *Postwar*, pp. 90–92.

the differing definitions of such terms as "democratic" and the four victors' greatly different security and political objectives in Europe. The allies' disharmony was eventually West Germany's opportunity. It permitted the Federal Republic of Germany (FRG) to rise rapidly from the ashes of defeat. However, talks involving the political and economic future of Germany stalled for a while, and American soldiers became impatient to go home. At the end of 1945 there were spontaneous GI demonstrations in Paris and Frankfurt that left no doubt in the minds of American leaders that the large part of the three million soldiers in Europe had to be demobilized without great delay. GIs were sent back to the US, and military and economic commitments to Europe were curtailed at a stunningly fast rate.

Between 1945 and 1947 the American defense budget sank by five-sixths. The US had ended the war in Europe with ninety-seven combat-ready ground divisions in the European theater; two years later, those had shrunk to only twelve divisions. Most were under strength or assigned to non-combat tasks. By the time that NATO had been agreed upon and signed by ten European countries, the US and Canada in April 1949, there were a total of 14 divisions remaining in Western Europe, of which a mere two were American. The Western allies were outnumbered on the ground by a ratio of twelve-to-one. Secretary of State Dean Acheson assured the Senate that the US would not deploy a significant number of ground troops in Europe. By December 1950, Defense Secretary Marshall suggested raising US forces in Europe to about four infantry divisions and the equivalent of one and one-half armored divisions, eight tactical air groups, and necessary naval forces. The JCS recommended approximately six divisions of ground forces. Further forces could be dispatched to Europe if hostilities broke out.[12]

---

12   Judt, *Postwar*, pp. 109, 150. *Marshall Papers*, Vol. 7, p. 286.

Military planning was based on the maximum of self-help of the Western European allies. Although that was a small fighting force, costing only 10 percent of the US defense budget, Marshall believed it would make a "tremendous morale contribution" to European security. This would be more important than the actual manpower figures. In Marshall's opinion, the "will to defend" and "the determination to fight if that be necessary" are important to "enable us to avoid war." Such a deterrence force "would help make free Europe hard to conquer" and "should give an imprudent aggressor something to think about before he dare set out on a hostile venture."[13]

Aware that peace in Europe depended heavily on America's nuclear deterrent, French Prime Minister René Pleven asked on a January 30, 1951, visit to Washington "whether the United States' predominance in the atomic field is being maintained." The president assured him that American advances in nuclear weapons were "phenomenal." Acheson confessed that there had been no discussion of the atom bomb, but that its retaliatory power and military potential were "immense." Marshall evaded the question.[14]

While searching for a way out of the dangerous Korean quagmire, Marshall, backed by the state and defense departments, consistently argued that America's foreign policy focus should remain on the primacy of defending Western Europe. On December 11, 1950, he said in a meeting of the National Security Council that the launching of NATO was close at hand. "Our entire international position depended on strengthening Western Europe. We could not rush into measures for Korea and the Pacific that would cause such Russian reactions that our European allies would be scared away." There was a consensus within the Truman administration: Europe First! Deputy Defense Secretary Robert

---

13   *Marshall Papers*, Vol. 7, p. 599 and documents 238, 239, 255.

14   *Marshall Papers*, Vol. 7, p. 358

Lovett summarized the consensus that "Korea is not a decisive area for us" and that although Korea is useful in defending Japan, "Western Europe was our prime concern."[15] Until the end of his tenures as secretary of state and defense, Marshall utilized every opportunity to remind listeners of this key point. "We should not become involved in fighting on the mainland of Asia," adding that "we should not lessen our efforts for the defense of Europe because of the Pacific." The United States could survive a loss of Korea, regrettable as that might be, but a Soviet victory in Western Europe, especially in Germany, would greatly endanger America's position in the world.[16]

America's allies agreed. In meetings with British Prime Minister Clement Attlee, December 4–8, 1950, Marshall and all others present agreed that the defense of Korea should be continued. But the defense of Europe remained the primary concern. Attlee agreed: "We must not get so involved in the East as to lay ourselves open to attack in the West." Dean Acheson added: "We must bear in mind that the central enemy is not the Chinese but the Soviet Union." Most Republicans disagreed with "Europe First" and initiated a "Great Debate" in Congress over the priorities in American defense policy. This prompted heated criticism of Marshall, but it did not alter his conviction.[17]

Marshall was at pains to emphasize to his countrymen that a significant American contribution to leadership within a Western European defense system was in the self-interest of the United States.

The defense of Europe was part of defending the US. "It would cost the US less, both in terms of men and of money, to

15 *Marshall Papers*, Vol. 7, document 198 and p. 276.

16 *Marshall Papers*, Vol. 7, document 330 and p. 577. Hitchcock, *Eisenhower*, pp. 49–52.

17 *Marshall Papers*, Vol. 7, documents 175, 210.

British Prime Minister Clement Attlee with Marshall, December 1950.

cooperate with the Europeans in the development of a unified force for the defense of Europe than to increase the number of United States divisions stationed in Europe above those now contemplated." Ten months later, he repeated that NATO is "a project of self-interest" and for this country, of the highest and most pressing urgency. Progress is being made by creating and strengthening of NATO.[18]

Marshall knew well that having allies is a critical asset for a credible defense of Europe. On February 15, 1951, he explained: "The US will be safer if friendly governments are

---

18 *Marshall Papers*, Vol. 7, document 122. First quote from Sept 22–23, 1950, his first meeting after swearing in. Also pp. 570, 572.

in power in the North Atlantic Community." They help the US avoid war. On July 27, 1951, he again maintained that "it would be unwise for us to rely solely upon our own strength. The most effective and least costly means of insuring peace is through mutual aid and collective security arrangements with our allies."[19]

Marshall acknowledged that American power does not rest on military means alone. "It is also measured by its qualities for leadership, by its resources and industries, by the determination of its people, and by the strength of its friends and allies. That is why we joined NATO and Rio Pact [for Latin America] and why Congress approved the Mutual Defense Assistance Act in 1949." In testimony before Congress on June 29, 1951, he asserted that NATO "is a project of self-interest for this country, of the highest and most pressing urgency." In 1949, the Senate approved NATO by a margin of eighty-two to thirteen and the Military Aid Program fifty-five to twenty-four. This was despite the fact that public opinion in America was clearly opposed to deploying a large number of US soldiers to Europe so soon after the Second World War and the dispensing of $12 billion in Marshall Plan assistance.[20]

None of this suggests that the United States should not defend South Korea. Secretary of State Acheson said on December 3, 1950: The "great problem is that we are fighting the wrong nation....The real enemy is the Soviet Union." Its threat of tyranny was growing. But he warned of the "danger of our becoming the greatest appeasers of all time if we abandon the Koreans and they are slaughtered."[21]

---

19   *Marshall Papers*, Vol. 7, documents 238, 239 and p. 598.

20   *Marshall Papers*, Vol. 7, documents 329, 238 and p. 570. Hitchcock, *Eisenhower*, p. 50.

21   *Marshall Papers*, Vol. 7, pp. 281 and 597.

In a December 19, 1950, meeting, when the US and its UN allies were being hit hard by motivated and hardened Chinese troops in the northern half of the Korean peninsula, Marshall asked "whether there was any way in which we could withdraw from Korea with honor." "Korea is not the place to fight a major war." General MacArthur bluntly disagreed![22]

Dean Rusk was persuaded that US credibility was at stake. The United States could not surrender in Korea. He continued: "We cannot sustain here the theory of an absolute priority for Europe if we surrender the Far East. Chairman of the JCS Omar Bradley asked if Europeans would believe the US would go to war with Soviets if it did not respond to a Chinese attack.[23]

Why was this focus on Europe hard for Americans to understand? Most Americans had anticipated that their troops would leave Europe as soon as the fighting was over at the end of the Second World War. President Roosevelt had said at the Yalta conference in February 1945 that occupation troops would remain in Germany two years at most. Truman was under powerful pressure to abide by this. An October 1945 poll taken of American voters revealed that only seven percent of respondents considered that foreign problems should be ranked ahead of domestic matters. Their knowledge of and interest in European affairs were severely limited. This rattled the European allies.[24]

America is a long way from the European continent. Lord Tedder remembered Marshall saying that Americans should imagine that European troops would be stationed permanently in the US under a European commander, and ask them to appreciate the sacrifices they would be called upon to bear. Also the European situation "is quite different from ours, in that

---

22   *Marshall Papers*, Vol. 7, pp. 316–17.

23   *Marshall Papers*, Vol. 7, p. 282.

24   Judt, *Postwar*, p. 109.

*Churchill, Roosevelt, and Stalin at the Yalta Conference,
February 1945. Marshall is middle rear.*

they are recovering from a devastating experience, both as to
personnel and as to their installations of one kind or other in
their countries. Just as they are beginning to lift themselves
out of that depression, there is imposed on them the necessity
for building up a very heavy charge against their economies for
purely military purposes. So they are in quite a critical state."[25]

The years 1949 through 1951 were crucial ones for the
formation and enlargement of the North Atlantic Treaty
Organization. As secretary of state from January 1947 until

---

25   *Marshall Papers*, Vol. 7, documents 289 and 330 and p. 577. Nevertheless,
     it was known that Marshall expected the allies to help pay for their
     defense. On his first full day as defense secretary, September 22, 1950,
     the *New York Post* chose as its headline: "Marshall to Allies: Put up!"

January 1949, Marshall was at the helm of US foreign policy during such crises as the Communist takeover of Czechoslovakia in February 1948 and the Berlin Airlift, which inspired the initial collective defense efforts. He had laid some of the groundwork that went into this unique peacetime alliance.

The Treaty of Brussels was signed by France, Britain, and the three BENELUX countries on March 17, 1948. It pledged the parties to render all "assistance in their power" to any partner that is attacked. The instrument to accomplish this was the Western European Union (WEU), which was mostly absorbed by NATO a year later.

The Truman administration accepted the need for a military alliance with the Western European democracies. The June 11, 1948, Vandenberg Resolution endorsed an "association of the United States" with "such regional and other collective arrangements as are based on continuous and effective self-help and mutual aid." The North Atlantic Treaty (aka Washington Treaty) was signed in Washington on April 4, 1949. Marshall's solid support of the alliance was hardly surprising, given the threatening international environment at the time. On March 5, 1951, he wrote that "it is not a peaceful world and when you are at the hub, it is pretty tough business." A month later, he added that "the best we can hope for in this present world of ours is a long period of tension." In a speech to the Foreign Policy Association on May 6, 1949, he stated: "This treaty, binding the signatory nations to protect the security of the North Atlantic area, is one of the most determined steps the United States has ever taken in its history." He saw it as an indispensable deterrent to war. A month and a half after retiring as secretary of defense, he told the Women's Patriotic Conference on National Defense: "War is abhorrent to me and I pray that we may avoid it, for I have lived with daily casualty lists and that is a truly awful experience. I have gone through hospital after hospital and viewed the human wreckage of war. Always I left with the feeling that we had failed miserably in our efforts to avert the cause for such sacrifices." NATO was ratified by the Senate on July 21, 1949, after Marshall had retired as secretary of state. Congress followed up with the Mutual Defense Assistance Program, which offered a billion dollars of military aid. The first shipments went out in the spring of 1950.[26]

Despite such assistance, NATO's military muscle at this point was more on paper than real. Only ten allied divisions were deployed on West German territory. These were little more than half the 18 divisions experts believed were needed merely to delay a Warsaw Pact attack, to say nothing of defending the line along the Rhine River. That would require an estimated fifty-four divisions. American deployments amounted to only one infantry division, three armored cavalry regiments, and two fighter/bomber groups. If reinforcements were needed, five divisions, three separate regiments, and eleven air wings could be drawn from the United States and Canada. Was such a modest American commitment enough? Field Marshal Bernard Montgomery stated on June 15, 1950, that "as things stand today and in the foreseeable future, there would be scenes of appalling and indescribable confusion in Western Europe if we were ever attacked by the Russians." He considered the two American divisions deployed in Germany to be the alliance's only combat-ready forces in Western Europe.[27]

The conviction that the North Atlantic allies were unprepared for the challenges they faced was dramatically tested when North Korea unleashed a massive attack against South Korea on June 25, 1950. This action soon dragged six of ten American Army divisions into the war on the peninsula just at a time when

---

26 Walter S. Poole, *The History of the Joint Chiefs of Staff (JCS)*, Volume IV, 1950–1952, pp. 179–80. Marshall quotes in *Words of George C. Marshall*, pp. 159, 165, 169, 176–77.

27 Poole, *JCS*, pp. 185, 187.

the partners were working on agreements on how to defend Western Europe from a Soviet attack. This distraction did not cause President Truman to change his "Europe first" approach in the Cold War. He later explained that "I had no intention of allowing our attention to be diverted from the unchanging aims and designs of Soviet policy. I knew that in our age, Europe, with its millions of skilled workmen, with its factories, and transportation network, was still the key to world peace."[28]

GERMANY IN NATO?

As the military disparity in Europe became increasingly worrisome, American leaders became convinced that US policy should shed its punitive aspects toward Germany and shift toward whole-hearted support of the democratic, economic, and military potential in Germany. Not France, but Germany, was chosen as the engine for European recovery. It was also chosen to be the centerpiece of the United States' counter-Soviet strategy. Germany's status was shifting from defeated enemy to partner. This called for an abolition of the Occupation Statute, the assigning of ambassadors to Germany, the admission of Germany as a full and equal partner of NATO, and an amnesty of all German war criminals in Allied custody.[29]

Among Marshall's most important tasks in a series of NATO meetings was to convince the allies, especially the French, that embracing German rearmament within the structure of NATO was in France's interest. This had to be done carefully. On December 26, 1950, Marshall bemoaned the effect that unfortunate publicity had on the German people, "who are human like the rest of us." Open discussion of Germany's role as

---

28 Harry S. Truman, *Years of Trial and Hope, 1946–1952.* Vol. 2 of *Memoirs by Harry S. Truman,* p. 380. Poole, *JCS,* p. 186.

29 Beevor, *Paris,* pp. 288–89. *Marshall Papers,* Vol. 7, documents 193, 240, 336. Judt, *Postwar,* p. 244.

A demoralized German population.

a buffer state between East and West and as a battleground for future wars in Europe could not help but intensify the already strong pacifism in the country.[30]

Exploring ways to close the gap in conventional military power between Eastern and Western Europe, the Joint Chiefs of Staff announced on May 2, 1950, that from the military point of view "the appropriate and early rearming of Western Germany is of fundamental importance." General Omar Bradley stated unmistakably on June 30, 1950, that "it is very unrealistic to continue to talk about building up the defenses of Western Europe without facing up to this subject of at least partially rearming Western Germany." The Defense Department was so convinced of the necessity of German rearmament that it developed a "one package" approach *vis-*

---

30   *Marshall Papers,* Vol. 7, document 193. Judt, *Postwar,* p. 153. Cray, *General,* p. 599.

à-vis the Western European nations: America would commit no additional forces to Europe or appoint a unified command until the allies accepted German rearmament. Marshall found this tactic to be heavy-handed and unhelpful. Later as secretary of defense he softened it.[31]

The policies of disarmament and demilitarization had to be scrapped or changed. Looking back, President Truman agreed that German participation could convert NATO's responsibility from "a rear-guard action" to "a defense in depth." There were no illusions about the task of persuading those Western nations, especially France, that had suffered enormously under the brutal German occupation only five years earlier that the perpetrators of that brutality should be rearmed. Marshall proved to be a key negotiator in achieving that goal. In his September 19, 1950, confirmation hearings, he was asked if he favored "arming western Germany, either as a police force or in a more extensive way." He answered cautiously: "I would hesitate to do that. I have not formed my own opinions because I have not heard any discussion other than what I have read in the newspapers." In fact, he was already a powerful proponent.[32]

But would the Germans themselves agree to rearm? Pacifism had gripped a people that had suffered greatly from a war their leader had inflicted on Europe. The US High Commissioner for Germany, John J. McCloy, was convinced that a majority of Germans did not desire rearmament. Their newly adopted Basic Law (constitution) forbade it. A barrage of cables came to Secretary of State Acheson from America's missions around Europe arguing for greater German participation in European defense. He noted: "The real question was not whether Germany should be brought into a general European defense system, but whether this could be done without disrupting everything else

---

31   Poole, *JCS*, pp. 195, 200.

32   Poole, *JCS*, pp. 191–92. Truman, *Years of Trial*, p. 253.

we were doing and giving Germany the key position in the balancing of power in Europe."[33]

Marshall was certain that the only way to close the gap that existed in military capabilities on the European continent was an integrated NATO force with a single commander, necessarily an American. General Dwight D. Eisenhower, Marshall's favorite to command the new NATO force, agreed. He wrote to Marshall on August 3, 1951, that he had become convinced of "the German strength that is vital to us." Both were well aware of the problems a commander would have in leading a multinational, multilingual force.[34]

The Western German government of Chancellor Konrad Adenauer was also increasingly interested in such a prospect, but for different reasons: as a means to regain the lion's share of German sovereignty after the disastrous Second World War. The Cold War had frozen the division of Germany. But it also provided the western part opportunities that the crafty Adenauer knew how to exploit for the benefit of his country. There were intense fears, shared by Marshall, that the Soviet Union sought direct or indirect domination over all of Europe. When NATO planners began working on plans for defending Western Europe, it was quickly apparent that the Western allies and smaller Western European countries alone could not provide the necessary forces. This was especially true since the United States had no intention at that time of permanently maintaining large numbers of American troops in Europe. Western European defense was conceivable only with the help of Germany. Plans were developed accordingly.

Adenauer listened very carefully to the message coming from Western capitals: "No NATO without Germany; no Germany without NATO." He reflected on his immediate goals of securing

---

33   Poole, *JCS*, pp. 193–94.

34   *Marshall Papers*, Vol. 7, document 143 and pp. 286, 620.

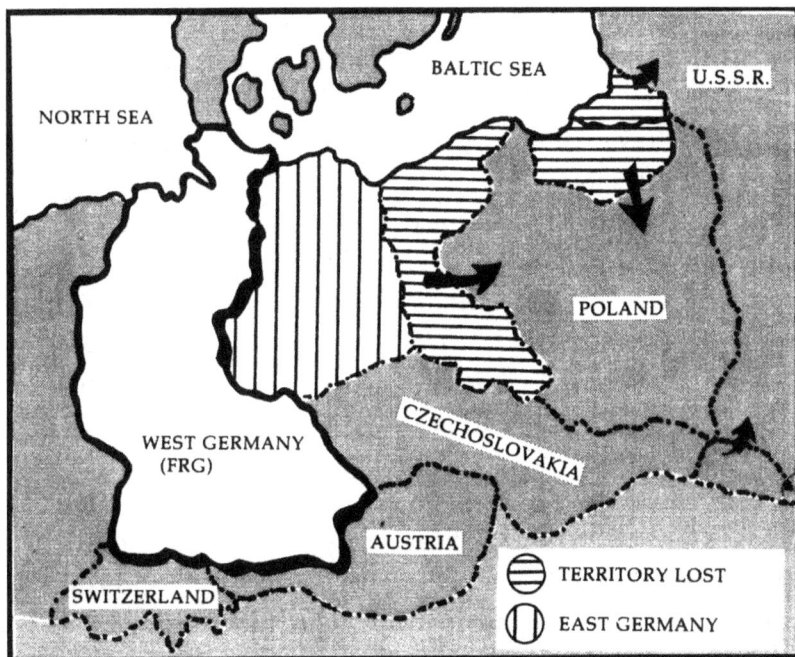

Germany after World War II. Courtesy of Rowman & Littlefield.

equality between Germany and other European countries, gaining full sovereignty for Western Germany, protecting his people from Soviet intervention, recovering from poverty and the ashes of disgrace, sharing again in international trade, rebuilding their devastated cities, and creating jobs for Germans.

He decided to strike a bargain with the NATO countries. On November 11, 1949, the 31st anniversary of the cease-fire ending World War I, Adenauer announced in an interview with the French newspaper, *L'Est Républicain,* that "if a common Supreme Command could be created, the Federal Republic would be willing at an appropriate time to integrate itself into a European defense system." He presented this decision to his own people as the "politics of necessity," and he stated the issue very simply: "We are faced with a choice between slavery and freedom. We choose freedom."

The State Department advocated a European Defense Force on August 16, 1950; it would allow German divisions to be integrated with non-German soldiers in corps and higher units. No German general staff would be permitted. This is an idea whose time did not come for another five years. However, on August 29, 1950, Chancellor Adenauer informed the High Commissioners that West Germany was ready to take part in a European Army.[35] In the years to come he was successful in getting an important political advantage for each increase in German activity or responsibility in NATO. He helped establish the United States as the permanent guarantor of West German security.

Adenauer succeeded in guiding his country into NATO despite daunting obstacles. First, the influential opposition Social Democratic Party of Germany (SPD) could not get out of its mind how this integration with the West, especially the military part of it, would affect the goal of German reunification. Most Germans at the time wanted this very much. It was an obligation placed on all West German governments by the framers of the 1949 Basic Law. That same Basic Law guaranteed that no German would be required to serve in the armed forces. Thus the creation of a new German army would require amending the Basic Law.

For years a majority of West Germans opposed the remilitarizing of their country. There was and still is a powerful pacifist strain in Germany that opposes all forms of German armament, especially nuclear weapons. This element was part of an emotional mass movement known by the slogan *Ohne mich*—without me. This movement enjoyed widespread support among the general population. For instance, one opinion survey in 1955 revealed that while 40 percent of respondents were in favor of a West German army, 45 percent were opposed. Among those identifying with the SPD, only 21 percent were in favor of

---

35   Poole, *JCS*, p. 195.

the *Bundeswehr* (Federal Army), and 71 percent were opposed. Nevertheless, the Federal Republic officially joined NATO in May 1955 and took into the newly created *Bundeswehr* the first thousand volunteer soldiers in January 1956.[36]

On September 8 and 11, 1950, just two weeks before Marshall took office as secretary of defense on September 21, a consensus had been reached within the administration that despite the war raging on the Korean peninsula, Europe remained the main theater of American concern. This conviction was strengthened by the dramatic victory at Inchon on September 15, which made the Korean War appear to be effectively over. In a letter dated September 25, 1950, Marshall wrote: "In assuming the duties of Secretary of Defense I have given my first attention to the pressing problems of achieving an adequate defense of the North Atlantic area."[37]

Therefore, additional US troops should be deployed on that continent as early as possible. They should constitute approximately four infantry divisions, the equivalent of one and a half armored divisions, eight tactical air groups, and appropriate naval forces. A European defense force within the North Atlantic Treaty framework that one day would include German soldiers would be the best means of achieving the maximum military contribution from European allies. An American Supreme Commander should be appointed if the European partners request that. President Truman accepted these proposals on September 11.[38]

---

36 Wayne C. Thompson, *Nordic, Central, & Southeastern Europe 2019–2020*, pp. 227–34. See also Wayne C. Thompson, *The Political Odyssey of Herbert Wehner*, pp. 118–25, 132–36.

37 George C. Marshall to Mr. Perkins, September 25, 1950, Correspondence, Box 195, Folder 36, George C. Marshall Library, Lexington, Virginia.

38 Poole, *JCS*, pp. 201–2.

Marshall agreed with everything the president had accepted. His tasks were enormous and urgent. He had to lift NATO to a level of efficiency to deter any Soviet temptations to attack Western Europe. He had to encourage America's allies on the continent to raise their commitment to defend themselves. He had to persuade them, especially France, to accept some form of German rearmament that would place limitations on the country that had menaced all of Europe only a few years before. He had to persuade the Germans to put aside their postwar pacifism and contribute militarily to a secure Europe. According to an opinion poll in the prestigious *Frankfurter Allgemeine Zeitung,* two out of three Germans (67 percent) strongly opposed German participation in Western defense. The alliance needed German manpower and industry, and an eastern NATO defensive line could not be defended without German assistance. He had to persuade Congress and the American people that a military commitment to Europe was in America's own interest as well as in the interest of the allies themselves.[39]

Marshall had to soften and make more flexible the "one-package" demand on France to accept Germans in the defense of the continent or risk losing an American military commitment to Europe. This would give French leaders more time to deliberate such a bold step so soon after the Second World War. Congress and the American public had to accept a unified command, led preferably by an American Supreme Allied Commander in Europe (SACEUR). All the time, he had to keep an eye on the war raging in Korea.

---

39   Condit, *Test,* pp. 317, 320–23, 309. Hitchcock, *Eisenhower,* p. 52–53.

CHAPTER FOUR

Marshall as Negotiator

MARSHALL WAS VERY CAREFUL TO DEFER TO THE AUTHORITY OF THE secretary of state, Dean Acheson, to take the lead in matters dealing with foreign policy, as opposed to military policy. Marshall played a key role in the series of foreign and defense minister meetings that began for him on September 22, 1950, the day after he was sworn into office. It was at that meeting that Acheson made the first formal proposal to rearm Germany as a western ally. Acheson himself described Marshall as of "immense help in two ways. His great prestige, calm, and compelling exposition left no doubt in any mind, including the French, that without Germany the defense of Europe was not possible." Acheson also became convinced himself. Marshall was able to persuade the Pentagon "that its previous insistence on a 'rigid and brusque one-package' proposal" that linked a united NATO command and increased US forces to German rearmament was counterproductive and "would not work."

The secretary of state also noted that Marshall "did useful work in private talks with [French Defense Minister] Jules Moch by getting him off generalities" and directing his attention to specifics, such as the matching of needs and resources. Moch had great admiration for Marshall; thus he was an avid listener to the general. In a speech to the Maryland Historical Society

*Marshall and Acheson with French Defense
Minister Jules Moch (second from right).*

on June 11, 1945, Marshall revealed an important key to success in negotiations: "It is very, very important to understand the other man's point of view. But, however much you disagree, if you understand the other man's point of view, you can usually work out a reasonable adjustment."[1]

Defense Minister Jules Moch, together with French Foreign Minister Robert Schuman, was the most important political figure in France and Marshall's chief interlocutor on German rearmament and NATO. A brilliant product of the prestigious Ecole Polytechnique, he had locked horns earlier with the powerful French Communist Party (PCF) as minister of the interior. A Socialist, he was Jewish and anti-clerical. He had hated the collaborationist Vichy State, and his family suffered terribly for its principles. His son was tortured

---

1   *Marshall Papers*, Vol. 7, pp. 167–68. Acheson, *Present*, p. 444. Marshall quote in *The Words of George C. Marshall*, p. 158.

to death by the Gestapo in a Nazi concentration camp for his activity in the French underground. In the opinion of one journalist, this tragedy made Moch "something of a fanatic about Germany." When it was suggested that this horrific personal loss influenced the advice he gave his government, he denied that this was the case.[2]

Secretary of State Acheson complained of Moch's "absolute intransigence" on the subject of German rearmament, a program, according to Moch, opposed by the French in a ratio of ten to one.[3] But cables from the US embassy in Paris described Moch in positive terms. He was "courageous"; his "energetic measures... tended to bolster the government's and his own prestige." As interior minister, he had put down a miners' strike. He energetically rooted out Communists from the police forces and CRS riot police. He actively opposed Communist union bosses, who had ordered their followers to demonstrate in the streets, to sabotage the economy and to destroy machinery in the factories.

The PCF, which won 29 percent of the votes in the November 1946 parliamentary elections, had declared its strong opposition to the Marshall Plan. The plan was not universally popular in France: in a mid-1950 poll, only one in three admitted that they had even heard of the plan, and 64 percent of the respondents believed it was bad for France. Another poll in France revealed that 47 percent were convinced that the Marshall Plan was dictated by America's desire to expand its markets. These negative views were all the more puzzling to Americans at a time when 150 ships a day were crossing the Atlantic in a logistical enterprise that exceeded anything like it during the Second World War.[4]

---

2   *Marshall Papers*, Vol. 7, document 130.

3   *Marshall Papers*, Vol. 7, documents 143, 130.

4   Judt, *Postwar*, p. 96. Beevor, *Paris*, p. 353. For two excellent studies of the Marshall Plan and postwar negotiations with the French, see Barry Machado, *In Search of a Usable Past: The Marshall Plan and*

Moch opposed such negative French opinions about the Marshall Plan. He believed that without it the government of Robert Schuman would never have succeeded in resisting the Communist onslaught. Both he and Schuman were firmly convinced that only a genuine improvement in the standard of living that the Marshall Plan had made possible could lessen the power of the Communists in the streets, the factories, and the ballot box.[5]

During his entire year in office, Marshall played a leading role in a series of top-level meetings. They began the day after he took the oath of office. The conference in New York City on September 22–23, 1950, brought together the "Big Three" (US, UK, France) foreign and defense ministers. The JCS recommended that Marshall push for an integrated defense force under a single commander and a nationally integrated staff. Subject to certain safeguards, German units should be included. At the meeting Marshall gave a blunt warning to Moch that Congress would reject funding for the rearmament of Europe if the French did not change their adamant refusal to accept some form of German military role. In the final communique, approved on September 26, some progress was noted. It approved of the early creation of "an integrated force adequate to deter aggression and ensure the defense of Western Europe, including Western Germany." The allies agreed to disagree on German rearmament until later.[6]

Postwar Reconstruction Today. Also Greg Behrman, *The Most Noble Adventure. The Marshall Plan and How America Helped Rebuild Europe.*

5   Beevor, *Paris*, pp. 299, 308–9.

6   Poole, *JCS*, pp. 205–7. Dean Acheson, *The Korean War*, p. 551. For the importance of German rearmament, see Stephen E. Ambrose, *Eisenhower: Soldier and President.* Marshall devoted much of his attention to Moch, who had expressed great admiration for him. However, the general was not an easy man to impress. Acheson

Marshall's challenge was to convince the allies, especially the French, that embracing German rearmament within the structure of NATO was in the French interest. It was also a precondition for a credible commitment by the United States to the defense of Western Europe. He sought to reduce the rigidity of the "one package" approach to rearming Germany and tying into European security as a way to make France more amenable. He asked the JCS on October 2 to come up with the concepts and practical measures needed to construct a European Defense Force (EDF). They should be "proposed in such a way as not to be contingent on German participation but adaptable to her inclusion." In other words, a gradual step-by-step piecemeal approach could be taken toward gaining French acquiescence. Marshall would utilize their ideas in subsequent NATO meetings.[7]

It would take until 1954 for the French government to accept the idea of putting weapons back into German hands. Some Frenchmen were already aware that there were positive aspects of NATO. American troops, however few in number, would be positioned between the Soviet Union and the Western European allies. Germany's inclusion in the alliance moved NATO's eastern border hundreds of miles eastward, thereby providing useful protection to France. Well trained and equipped NATO troops could also help reassure that Germany would not rearm itself outside the alliance and seek revanchist goals not shared by the allies. NATO's first Secretary General, Major General Lord Hastings Ismay, expressed this reassurance in this way: The

---

remembered Marshall's legendary reserve that bordered on aloofness. He "conveyed intensity, which his voice low, staccato, and incisive reinforced. It compelled respect. It spread a sense of authority and calm." James Chace, *Acheson: The Secretary of State Who Created the American World*, pp. 159, 161.

7   Poole, *JCS*, pp. 209–10.

purpose of NATO is "to keep the Russians out, the Americans in and the Germans down." Its very uniqueness as the first and only integrated allied command in peacetime the world had ever known was appealing.[8] Another appealing aspect for France, which was in the process of recovery from the recent world war and involved in a costly war in Indochina, was that it would receive assistance in equipping and expanding its own battered military forces.

On October 9, 1950, State, Defense, and Treasury Department officials met to discuss Marshall's view on how to convince future allies and how financial assistance could be offered to help them. Marshall expressed "serious reservations" about the Pentagon's "one package" approach to the French reluctance to rearm Germany. He concurred with the argument of Paul Nitze, head of the State Department's Policy Planning Staff, that "the successful defense of Europe was an integral part of the defense of the United States and that it would cost the United States less, both in terms of men and of money, to cooperate with Europeans in the development of a unified force for the defense of Europe than to increase the number of United States divisions stationed in Europe above those now contemplated."[9]

A State-Defense working group was also charged with reexamining potential positions on German rearmament. It agreed that committing American forces to West Germany's defense without German participation was impractical. They discussed ways to mitigate French fears of a German resurgence, such as limiting German divisions to one-fifth of the total, allowing Germans only to control administrative and logistically functions, and imposing limits or prohibitions on German industry. Germany would have neither a national army nor

---

8   Judt, *Postwar*, pp. 150–53.

9   *Marshall Papers*, Vol. 7, document 122. Condit, *Test*, p. 324.

a general staff. Marshall was not satisfied with this analysis, remarking that it states only "conditions for German participation without specifying how these were to be achieved." Marshall wanted more practical and detailed arrangements for integrating German military units into a European defense force.[10]

The JCS submitted a revised set of recommendations that, for example, called for attaching West German battalions and smaller units to American units in Germany if the NATO Defense Committee became deadlocked. The JCS also recommended that a Supreme Allied Commander in Europe be selected. It suggested that General Dwight D. Eisenhower, then president of Columbia University, be appointed. President Truman met with the general, and both were agreeable to the idea.[11]

In preparing for a visit by Moch to Marshall on October 16, 1950, a State Department briefing paper advised Marshall that Moch was getting more and more irritated by the notion of German rearmament and that his antipathy was so strong that he might resign from the French government if need be. It recommended that Marshall emphasize to the French defense minister the safeguards that were being discussed to contain an armed Germany. Also the French must realize that if they wanted the defense line to be located as far east as possible, it must accept that German soldiers would make that possible.

Moch continued to express his distrust of Germany, arguing that a rearmed Germany would ultimately side with the USSR as the stronger military power in Europe. He maintained that West German troops would never fight against their brethren in East Germany. He requested that any decision about German rearmament be postponed, threatening that France would reject it if it were put on the table at the forthcoming NATO Defense

10   Poole, *JCS*, p. 210. Condit, *Test*, p. 324.

11   Condit, *Test*, pp. 324–25. Poole, *JCS*, p. 210.

Committee meeting scheduled for October 28–31. Marshall countered that the United States would have to have an answer to the German situation by October 28. The meeting ended without agreement.[12]

In order to give the French parliament time to consider German rearmament within a NATO defense force, Marshall and his fellow defense ministers agreed to postpone the full NATO defense ministers meeting from October 16–20 to October 28–31. He continued to meet with Moch and to correspond with British Defense Minister Emmanuel Shinwell in an effort to narrow the differences among the allies.[13]

Before they could reconvene, French Premier René Pleven delivered a speech before parliament on October 24, 1950. He was uneasy about a rearmed Germany, but he was under allied pressure to find a place for German soldiers in western defense. He overwhelmingly rejected direct German participation in NATO on a divisional level and opposed any kind of German army and general staff. Instead the premier presented what became known as the "Pleven Plan." It called for an immediate appointment of a NATO supreme commander, and all combat troops would be assigned to his command. France would provide twenty divisions by 1954. A new experimental force under a European defense minister would be created. This minister would be outside of NATO and would answer to a future European Assembly that would be linked to the emerging European Coal and Steel Community (ECSC), the brain child of Jean Monnet.

This European army would be composed of French cadres and an equal number of French and German soldiers. No German units would be above the company or battalion level. In a subsequent meeting with Marshall, Moch was adamant that German divisions would be "tantamount to a German

---

12   Condit, *Test*, p. 325.

13   *Marshall Papers*, Vol. 7, document 143.

army." Insisting on it would cause the collapse of the French cabinet. Operational and trained units would be transferred to NATO command. Marshall had what was reportedly a "friendly, relaxed, and informal" conversation about the plan, but Moch would not budge.[14]

This plan baffled Marshall, as well as Acheson and the president. Marshall admitted that "we had been unable to penetrate the miasma of the French plan and discern any clear details." It was "so nebulous that no common ground could be said to exist." JCS Chairman Omar Bradley found it "entirely impractical." Germans would see their role as mere cannon fodder. A European minister of defense would make NATO inoperable. Acheson asserted that the plan "caused us consternation and dismay." Marshall agreed with him that it was "hopeless." British Defense Minster Shinwell found the plan "disgusting and nauseous" and called it "military folly and political madness." He threatened that it could cause the UK to withdraw its troops from the European continent.[15]

The idea of a European Defense Community (EDC) with its own European Defense Force (EDF) that would integrate German soldiers into an overall European command did not survive long. This was true even though this treaty was signed May 27, 1952, and was ratified by the West German parliament *(Bundestag)* in March 1953. Britain refused to join, and French public opinion gradually turned against it. The National Assembly, not wanting French troops to be under supranational control, rejected the proposal on August 30, 1954. After the vote the Gaullist and Communist deputies stood up and sang the *Marseillaise* national anthem. Nevertheless, within a year

14   *Marshall Papers*, Vol. 7, document 143. Condit, *Test*, pp. 326–27.

15   *Marshall Papers*, Vol. 7, document 143. Poole, *JCS*, pp. 211–12. Judt, *Postwar*, p. 244. André Fontaine, *History of the Cold War: From the Korean War to the Present*, pp. 39–49.

France overcame its worst fears and accepted West Germany's entry into NATO.

As host and chair of the NATO defense minister meeting in Washington that opened October 28, 1950, Marshall called again for the creation of a viable NATO defense force. Unaware of the military disaster American and UN troops would soon suffer in Korea, he stated that "victory in Korea is impressive evidence that the determined efforts of United Nations will have the backing of powerful military, naval, and air forces to defend the peace of the world." The military gap in Europe could only be closed by German rearmament within a unified NATO military force and under a single commander. Marshall admitted that rearming Germany posed a greater threat to Europe than to the US. Many French at the time also feared that German rearmament could provoke a Soviet attack.[16]

In order to create the basis for a compromise, Marshall scrupulously avoided criticizing the ill-fated Pleven Plan or pushing an American proposal. He assured the French that the US would continue to provide assistance in Indochina. At the same time, he believed that any plan the allies adopted would have to be realistic militarily and assure sufficient defensive capability. Since Moch continued to defend the Pleven Plan vigorously, action was postponed without agreement until the December meeting. Acheson blamed the failure to reach consensus on the "absolute intransigence of Moch."[17]

Scarcely had the ministers returned home when on November 3 the Soviet Union called for a conference of the four occupation powers to discuss the 1945 Potsdam agreement to unify and demilitarize Germany. Many Germans and French showed interest in such a situation, but Marshall, Acheson, and

---

16   *Marshall Papers*, Vol. 7, document 143.

17   *Marshall Papers*, Vol. 7, documents 129, 143 and pp. 358–59. Condit, *Test*, pp. 327–28, 330. Poole, *JCS*, p. 213.

Truman did not. They viewed it as a "Soviet spoiling operation." Nevertheless, seventy-four meetings of the four wartime allies took place before ending in deadlock. This failure underscored yet again that European security would have to depend upon the success of NATO.[18]

In the lead-up to the North Atlantic Council meeting in London scheduled for December 18–19, 1950, the search for a workable NATO alliance continued. General Eisenhower wrote Marshall on November 12 expressing reluctance in seeming to rush the United States into responsibility in Europe without a careful evaluation of the situation. Marshall answered that he shared that concern. Eisenhower wrote of the need to designate an American commander who would be present to deal with issues that need to be settled. He wrote that it would be very difficult to get twelve countries to "give carte blanche" to a Supreme Commander in peacetime. The German question is of great importance, but that will only come when the German people agree to it. A tremendous job has to be done to sell it to the German people and government. Marshall wrote back to Eisenhower: "If the problem can be solved, you are the one to solve it."[19]

Ambassador Charles M. Spofford submitted a plan bearing his name to deal with the conflict between French talk of an eventual European federation and the US desire for immediate German rearmament. He proposed the recruitment of Germans to serve in 5,000-man regimental combat teams while Europeans continued their discussion of common political institutions. German rearmament would thereby ultimately be achieved within the framework of a European army. The JCS accepted this plan with reservation. Division-size German units were necessary, but they could not be contingent upon the creation of

---

18   Condit, *Test*, pp. 338–39. Acheson, *Korean War*, p. 551.

19   George C. Marshall to General Eisenhower, November 1950. Correspondence 195/53, Marshall Library.

a French-led European federation. Also the time for bilingual military units had not yet come.[20]

In the State-Defense meeting on December 1, 1950, all participants agreed that future NATO conferences would be futile unless German participation were guaranteed in advance. In response Marshall made "an abrupt, authoritative statement that it was no use talking about divisions, integrated forces or commanders until we faced and solved the problem of whether we wished to moderate our present determined [one-package] stand."[21]

In the midst of this continuing discussion Chinese troops launched a massive and unforeseen attack against American and UN forces moving north in Korea. This temporarily dominated discussion and affected planning for the US presence in Europe. In the National Security Council Marshall elaborated the government's "Europe first" policy: "Our entire international position depended on strengthening Western Europe. We could not rush into measures for Korea and the Pacific that would cause such Russian reactions that our European allies would be scared away." The JCS added that "both our obligations in the Far East and our military commitments under NATO can be realized."[22]

Citing the dramatic turn of events in Korea, Acheson appealed to French Foreign Minister Robert Schuman to end the standoff in light of the "dangerous drift of German opinion." In part to clarify a careless remark by Truman on the possible use of atomic weapons in Korea, British Prime Minister Clement Attlee traveled to Washington from December 4 to 8, 1950, to confer with the president, Marshall, and Acheson.

20   *Marshall Papers*, Vol. 7, p. 286. Poole, *JCS*, pp. 213–14.

21   Condit, *Test*, p. 331. Poole, *JCS*, pp. 214–17.

22   Poole, *JCS*, p. 215.

The Americans assured Attlee that the primary American concern was Europe, and the main enemy was the Soviet Union. However, Marshall noted that the US had planned to deploy three divisions to Germany in the course of 1951, but the turn of events in Korea made this "very problematical." He was adamantly opposed to sending untrained and unprepared troops into a war zone.[23]

To reassure French Foreign Minister Robert Schuman, US Ambassador to France, David Bruce, recommended that the US send him a letter providing public evidence of its firm American support for the French proposals. The French cabinet strongly desired such a reassuring letter, which could make Paris more amenable to German rearmament. Both Marshall and Acheson favored such an important gesture to the French allies. The letter was sent December 7, 1950. The French were willing to put aside their hopes for a European army. This ended the deadlock over arming the Germans.[24]

It was agreed that safeguards against a resurgence of German militarism would be kept in place as long as they were deemed necessary. They included initially a limit on unit size to regimental combat teams, which the new supreme commander could use as he judged best. German airplanes would be part of NATO's air forces. A German army would be administered by civilians, and there would be no general staff. Its contribution should not exceed 20 percent of the troops assigned to the integrated force.[25] Not until May 5, 1955, did western Germany formally enter NATO, and it swore in its first volunteers on January 1, 1956.

---

23 For Truman's public misstatement about the possible use of nuclear weapons in Korea, see Pogue, *Marshall*, pp. 464, 468, and DavidHalberstam, *The Coldest Winter: America and the Korean War*, pp. 478–79.

24 Condit, *Test*, pp. 332–33

25 Poole, *JCS*, pp. 218–19. Condit, *Test*, pp. 332–33.

NATO's military Committee convened in London on December 12, 1950, and agreed to create an integrated European defense force within NATO, a supreme headquarters and the reorganization of the military structure. This meeting prepared the way for the NATO meetings in Brussels December 18–19, 1950, when these decisions were adopted. Marshall was fully involved in the essential remake of NATO. However he decided not to leave Washington for the December meetings in Europe because of the grim situation in Korea. Instead Secretary of the Army Frank Pace accompanied Secretary of State Acheson.

Marshall and Deputy Secretary Lovett had a meeting with General Eisenhower on December 14 to discuss the latter's appointment as NATO supreme commander. They assured him that the JCS fully agreed that all US forces in the area would be under his command when needed. Eisenhower was aware that the NATO force would not be sizable for a while, but his importance for the fledgling alliance was clear. Lovett asserted that Ike would be the kind of supreme commander around whom Europe could rally.[26]

As the year 1950 ended, Marshall could look back on impressive progress in strengthening the NATO alliance. American forces had been significantly augmented in western Europe. The signs were good that America's European partners would fulfill their promises and match the United States' efforts. The US Seventh Army, under the command of Lieutenant General Manton S. Eddy, was activated in western Germany in November 1950. General Eisenhower's appointment as SACEUR was formally announced on December 19, and President Truman stated in a press conference that even more troops would be sent to Europe although their numbers had yet to be decided.[27]

---

26   Condit, *Test*, p. 333.

27   Poole, *JCS*, p. 221.

Discussions continued in Washington with French Premier René Pleven on January 29 and 30, 1951, involving Marshall, Acheson, President Truman, and others. Pleven assured the president that France continued to support German economic and military integration. He asked bluntly if the United States had the capability to defend Europe with nuclear weapons in the event that the Soviet Union would attack before NATO had completed its buildup. He pointedly asked "whether the United States' predominant position in the atomic field is being maintained." Truman assured him "that our advance in the atomic field was phenomenal." Acheson stated that there had been no discussion of the atomic bomb, but that the US possessed "terrific and immediate retaliatory power" in the US. Its military potential was "immense." Marshall added that the rapid buildup of military strength in Europe was the only alternative to submission to the Russians. He was pleased at the premier's commitment to have an army of nine hundred thousand soldiers by 1953.[28]

AMERICAN TROOPS IN EUROPE

The historic decision to send a large number of American soldiers during peacetime sparked an outcry in Congress and the public that was so angry that many termed it "the great debate." In some ways this recalled the emotional controversy in 1940 and 1941 over the provision of American military assistance to the United Kingdom. Republican Senator Robert A. Taft called for a complete "re-examination of foreign policy," while former President Herbert Hoover advocated that America's energies be redirected toward preserving a "Western Hemisphere Gibraltar of Western Civilization." The debate even extended to whether the president has the authority to send troops abroad in time of peace. Senator Kenneth S. Wherry found it appropriate to

---

28 *Marshall Papers*, Vol. 7, document 223.

introduce a proposal in Congress on January 8, 1951, worded: "Resolved that no ground forces...should be assigned to duty in the European [theater]...ending the formulation of a policy with respect thereto by the Congress."[29]

This claim that Congress had a say in any subsequent increase of American troop strength in Europe was unacceptable to President Truman. His view was that as commander-in-chief he was authorized "to send troops anywhere in the world." As far as Congress was concerned, he declared in a January 13 press conference: "I don't ask their permission, I just consult them."[30]

On February 2, 1951, Senator William F. Knowland sent Eisenhower a list of questions relevant to the upcoming Senate hearings on America's deployment of troops in Europe. Ike passed the letter on to Marshall, who addressed the questions the senator had posed. The defense secretary confirmed that General Eisenhower as SACEUR would consult with allied governments before deploying their soldiers across national frontiers. In time of war, the SACEUR would have exclusive control of armed forces assigned to him.

Marshall stated that the alliance had about 2,300,000 land forces in being, of which 215,000 were stationed in Germany. They faced seventy-three Soviet divisions in European Russia, thirty in the Eastern European satellite states and eastern Germany, and fifty-one in Siberia. In addition, the satellite states had their own divisions. He noted that there were uncertain factors: Could allied intelligence agencies provide adequate advance warning of an intended Soviet attack? Might there be effective guerrilla warfare inside Soviet-held territory? What position would Yugoslavia take? The most important unknown involved West Germany: would it provide the military, political,

---

29   Poole, *JCS*, pp. 221–2. Acheson, *Present*, pp. 460, 489–93.

30   Poole, *JCS*, p. 222. Condit, *Test*, p. 341.

and psychological forces essential for the defense of its own territory?[31]

A delegation of German leaders visited Marshall on February 15, 1951, the day his Senate testimony began. He commented that such a grilling probably had never been held in Germany, eliciting a laugh from the visitors. The Germans in the delegation assured Marshall that Germany was definitely on the side of the West. But they explained that the Occupation Statute prevented their country from making a military contribution to their own defense. Lifting these limitations would strengthen Germans' confidence and morale.[32]

Marshall gave the opening testimony in the Senate committee's joint hearings on February 15, 1951. As always he approached this task of dealing with Congress in an admirable way, according to Charles E. Bohlen. "He would never lie or deceive senators or representatives. He would never tell questioners at the hearings that they had no right to information or that it was too sensitive. Instead of saying no, he would suggest that the hearing go into closed session, where he would be completely candid with them. His third rule was to study the backgrounds of senators and representatives carefully so that he understood not only the questions they asked but why they were asking them."[33] As secretary of defense, Marshall worked hard on congressional relations. He testified sixteen times on defense legislation, and he remained in constant contact with leaders of both parties.

Marshall argued that by upping American power in Europe, the US would deter aggression and at the same time would help friendly governments remain in power. All of this would

---

31   Marshall Library, Xerox 2569, Box 3.

32   *Marshall Papers,* Vol. 7, documents 240, 295, 329.

33   Charles E. Bohlen, *Witness to History, 1929–1969,* pp. 270–71.

enhance America's own security. Marshall pleaded for an increase of strength on the ground in Europe. With the backing of the president, he revealed the administration's plan to deploy four additional divisions in Europe; this would make a total presence of six divisions or approximately 100,000 soldiers. Such specifics about future troop deployments were unprecedentedly open to the Soviets. Marshall contended that the conclusions of such a great national debate should not rest on uncertainties. This unexpectedly small size of actual commitment took some of the steam out of the opposition. However, he was against permitting Congress to place limits on the exact number of divisions to be deployed.[34]

In Acheson's view, the testimony of the secretary of defense was achieved with "devastating effect." The same can be said about that delivered by General Eisenhower and General Lucius Clay. Ike was so impressed with Clay's presentation that he considered it to have been superior to both Marshall's and General Bradley's. He feared that the congressional troop restrictions would endanger his NATO command. He reportedly said that "I cannot escape the fervent wish that he [Clay] were our secretary of defense."[35]

Marshall had written a letter to Ike on November 12, 1950, addressing it in his customary way: "Dear Eisenhower." He shared Ike's reluctance to rushing the US into military responsibility in Europe without a careful evaluation of the situation. Most vitally, no viable defense could be mounted until "the German people agree to it." "A tremendous job [is] yet to be done to sell it to the German people and the German government." He acknowledged the great difficulty of getting a dozen countries to give carte blanche to a foreign supreme commander in peacetime. But Marshall expressed certainty that if the problems could be

---

34   Chace, *Acheson*, p. 328. Condit, *Test*, pp. 340–41.

35   Condit, *Test*, p. 341.

Marshall making a point at a congressional hearing.

solved, Ike was the one to solve them.[36]

On April 4, 1951, Congress approved by a vote of 69–21 the deployment to Europe of the four divisions that the administration had decided upon. At the same time, it approved

36   Marshall Library correspondence 195/53.

the appointment of General Eisenhower as NATO supreme commander. However, it also asserted as "the sense of the Senate" that no additional ground forces should be sent to Europe without prior Congressional consent. Both Congress and the administration claimed victory, but Truman got his way. The last ground units arrived in Germany on December 8, 1951, after Marshall had stepped down from office. The air wings reached Germany between June and October of that year. This was a significant victory for President Truman and Secretary Marshall. Their plans for defending Western Europe were no longer seriously questioned during the remainder of the Truman presidency.[37]

Difficult negotiations continued in Paris over the creation of some form of European Army and in Bonn with Chancellor Konrad Adenauer over the conditions of German rearmament. Marshall strongly recommended that the French be kept fully informed of all discussions with the Germans to avoid delays and any form of embarrassment to the French. In the meantime the complicated talks with Bonn should proceed "in a steadfast, orderly manner." "It is my feeling that we should seek to have a comprehensive German proposal at an early date."[38]

As he often did, Marshall requested that the Joint Chiefs of Staff provide him with comments and suggestions. They rejected a unified neutral Germany and were skeptical of a European Army, with its cumbersome chains of command and lines of communication. But Eisenhower found such a European force acceptable. At a joint State-Defense conference on July 16, 1951, Marshall requested and Acheson accepted that the secretary of state would prepare a recommendation for approval by President Truman. On July 30, the two secretaries completed their conclusions and recommendations for German participation

---

37   Chace, *Acheson*, pp. 328–9. Poole, *JCS*, p. 224.

38   *Marshall Papers*, Vol. 7, documents 295, 329.

in Western European defense and ultimate full membership in NATO. Truman approved on August 2, 1951. It would take several years to achieve the integration of German troops in NATO. But the allies had embarked on that difficult course by 1951, in the closing months of Marshall's tenure as secretary of defense.[39]

While Marshall was wrestling with the difficult diplomatic problems involving the defense of Europe, the war in Korea had taken several dangerous turns for the worse. It sometimes appeared that retreating American and UN troops could be driven off the Korean peninsula. The secretary of defense continued to give all he had to prevent a limited war in Asia from becoming an all-out conflict in China or Europe.

---

39   Poole, *JCS*, pp. 257–58, 260–64.

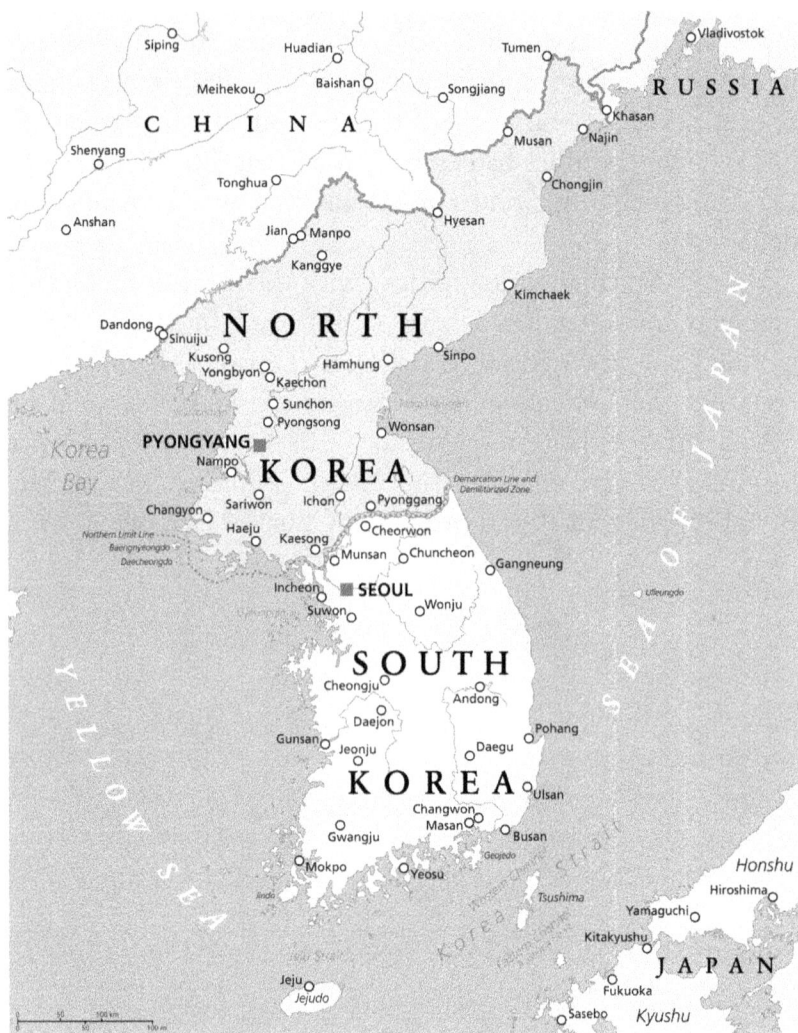

Map of Korea. Courtesy of Getty Image/Peter Hermes Furian.

CHAPTER FIVE

Marshall and the Korean War

IN THE CLOSING HOURS BEFORE DAWN ON JUNE 25, 1950, TROOPS FROM Communist-ruled North Korea stormed southward across the 38th parallel. They had advanced largely undetected to this line that divided the Korean peninsula. Their objective: to capture the whole of South Korea in a matter of weeks and to unify all of Korea under Communist rule. Taking full advantage of the element of surprise, the North Koreans moved quickly through South Korean territory and captured the southern capital of Seoul on the second day of their well-prepared and planned attack. However, they failed to achieve their goal of a rapid surrender of the Republic of Korea (ROK) government led by Syngman Rhee.

Japan had annexed Korea in 1910. At the end of World War II in August 1945, American soldiers, who had landed at Inchon in September 1945, a few miles from Seoul, and Soviet troops were on Korean territory. The two world war allies were in a hurry to disarm the Japanese soldiers and to repatriate back to Japan all Japanese military and civilians, numbering an estimated 700,000 persons. To facilitate the surrender and transfer of Japanese troops, the US and Soviet Union divided the country along the 38th parallel in the final week of World War II. This was to be a temporary line until a high-level peace conference could agree on the Korea's future as a unified country. The 38th parallel had never existed as a line of demarcation separating two Korean states.[1] As was the case in Germany, such a summit never took place as the cold war replaced the earlier world war.

Doubtful that a settlement could be achieved within a reasonable time, President Harry S. Truman persuaded the newly established United Nations to take over responsibility for Korea in 1947 even though US forces maintained control in the South for another year. The UN adopted resolutions calling for Korean unity, but nothing was done to enact them despite elections in the South on May 10, 1948. The then Secretary of State George C. Marshall stated that the fact that 90 percent of registered voters had participated showed that South Koreans "are determined to form their own government by democratic means." The Soviets announced in early 1949 that they had withdrawn their troops from the North, and General Douglas MacArthur followed suit by recommending the same for American troops. They were gone by the end of June 1949. While secretary of state, Marshall had supported this action although he warned against too rapid a withdrawal from Korea, fearing that it could prompt a Communist takeover. He said on September 29, 1949, when he was no longer secretary of state, that "ultimately the US position in Korea is untenable even with the expenditure of considerable US money and effort."[2] The United States combat capability had been neglected since the Second World War, much of its equipment had become antiquated, and there were three well-armed enemies in the region: North Korea, China, and the Soviet Union.

At the time of the June 1950 attack, the US had a military presence of only a few political and military advisers. The poorly

---

1   David McCullough, *Truman*, p. 785. Pogue, *Marshall*, p. 442.

2   Pogue, *Marshall*, pp. 444–46. Clay Blair, *The Forgotten War: America in Korea, 1950–1953*, pp. 40–46. Quote on p. 41.

trained and equipped South Korean forces were no match for the approximately 109,000 or seven divisions of well-equipped and battle-tested northern attackers. They outnumbered their southern counterparts almost two-to-one, and about half had combat experience. The latter moved so fast in two separate columns that they encircled entire South Korean units while heading toward the southern port of Pusan. There a hastily constructed defense perimeter sought to prevent a North Korean takeover of the entire peninsula and a forced evacuation of the remaining American personnel.[3]

Truman acted quickly by instructing General MacArthur to supply the ROK army with munitions and to muster sufficient air power to protect US citizens if an evacuation became necessary. Arguing that time was of the essence, President Truman did not seek a declaration of war from the US Senate, later describing it as a "police action." He turned to the United Nations on June 25, 1950, to demand a halt to the invasion. Two days later, he sought UN approval of military assistance. Due to a fortuitous Soviet absence in protest against the refusal to seat the newly proclaimed People's Republic of China (PRC), the American proposals were adopted with a minimum of dissent. The vote in the Security Council was nine in favor and one abstention. The US went to war supported by fifteen allies.

Truman's team, which did not yet include the retired Marshall, debated what the enemy's intentions were and what should be done about it. Was the hidden hand of Stalin's Soviet Union at work? What role might the newly victorious Chinese Communists be playing? Truman declared that "I don't want to go to war," but he felt the necessity to send American ground forces to South Korea, drawn initially from Japan and Okinawa. He explained to a group of congressmen invited to the White House: "The attack upon Korea makes it plain beyond all doubt

---

3   Halberstam, *Coldest Winter*, p. 54.

that communism has passed beyond the use of subversion to conquer independent nations and will now use armed invasion and war."

Putting aside his notes, the president delivered a sweeping impromptu analysis: The attack "was very obviously inspired by the Soviet Union. If we let Korea down, the Soviets will keep right on going and swallow up one piece of Asia after another. We have to make a stand some time or else let all of Asia go. If we were to let go, the Near East would collapse and no telling what would happen in Europe. Therefore I have ordered our forces to support Korea as long as we can—or as long as the Koreans put up a fight and give us something we can support." The American public supported this decision.[4]

Marshall agreed that the US should not practice appeasement in Korea. In a statement he made for the United Nations Day Program on October 24, 1950, he said that "a blow at freedom anywhere is a blow at freedom everywhere." He also shared the

---

4   H.W. Brands, *The General vs. the President: MacArthur and Truman at the Brink of Nuclear War*, pp. 85–86. For Marshall's views on nuclear weapons in the Cold War, see Frank A. Settle, Jr., *General George C. Marshall and the Atomic Bomb*, especially pp. 175–86. As secretary of defense, Marshall was responsible for nuclear weapons. He insisted on civilian authority over them and that control should rest with the president, not the military. He was aware that the president and JCS considered using nuclear bombs in Korea in the summer of 1950. But such weapons were not useful in the mountainous terrain. Truman ordered preparations for a nuclear attack if the Soviet Union entered the war. See also Bland, *George C. Marshall*, pp. 421–25: Marshall strongly opposed their use in the Korean War. However, during the Second World War he had been deeply involved in all aspects of the preparation and use of the atomic bomb. He amassed the money and manpower for its development. He regarded its use to force Japan to end the war as "of great importance." "I think it was quite necessary to drop the bomb in order to shorten the war....There were hundreds and hundreds of American lives involved in this thing." The bloody capture of Okinawa, when Japanese troops fought to the death and sacrificed 120,000 soldiers, was fresh in his mind.

president's determination that a war in Korea be a limited one, not an Asia-wide or world war. A military commitment to Korea had to be weighed against the overriding need to support the newly created North Atlantic Treaty Organization in Europe. During the entire conflict in Korea both Marshall and Truman were convinced that the key arena for American security lay in Europe, not Asia.[5]

Marshall knew a lot about Korea. As Chief of Staff in the last weeks of the Second World War, he had taken part in critical decisions affecting that peninsula. This included the drawing of the 38th Parallel separating North Korea from South Korea and the creation of the forerunner to the US Military Advisory Group for South Korea. During his one-year assignment in China, he greatly enhanced his commitment to and understanding of Asian affairs.[6]

The Truman team wanted to tap this valuable source of insights even before Marshall had been named secretary of defense. George Kennan wrote in his diary that on July 1, 1950, Secretary of State Dean Acheson had proposed that he, Averell Harriman, Chip Bohlen, and Kennan go to Leesburg to have a discussion with Marshall. The latter invited them for lunch, and the group went to Leesburg immediately, conducting their meeting on the lawn. "The general was in fine form." He "listened very attentively and silently, as he always does when a problem is being exposed before him, and then he gave us his views vigorously and with hesitation." He admitted that his statements were based on "very scanty information."

Marshall said that "there could be no doubt about the proper course for us to pursue. We had begun this thing; now we had

---

5   *Marshall Papers*, Vol. 7, documents 138, 142. Pogue, *Marshall*, pp. 450–51. MacArthur called limited war "appeasement." Unger, *Marshall*, p. 474.

6   Pogue, *Marshall*, p. 441.

to go through with it. His greatest worry had been that for the sake of Korea we might have risked an alienation of public opinion in Western Europe, which was the area of the greatest real strategic importance." Kennan wrote that Marshall was "deeply disturbed over what he understood to be the attitudes in the Defense Establishment, particularly with their relation to the Department of State." He did not feel that we needed to send more in the way of military support to MacArthur. It was a common failing of commanders in the field to ask for more than they needed, and MacArthur was far from being an exception to this rule. He should be told to do this job with what he had. He could do it if he applied himself to it. The depletion of the forces on Japan was not dangerous. Any amphibious action against Japan would be a great undertaking, and a very risky one in the face of any sizeable air and naval defense. He was particularly concerned about the initial tendency of the Air Force to think that they could do this all alone. That, he said, was the same old thing. The Air Force and the Navy were full of ideas about how they could do things."[7] Truman followed up this informative visit with one of his own to Marshall's home in Leesburg three days later on July 4, 1950.

Unfortunately the US had precious little to deploy. It had hollowed out its military forces to an astonishing extent after the Second World War, from twelve million men and women at the end of the war to only 1.5 million by the beginning of 1947; 15,000 soldiers were demobilized per day. This was accompanied by a precipitous decline in the defense budget. By the time the Korean War had broken out in June 1950, the US was left with an army that "could not fight its way out of a paper bag," in the words of General Omar Bradley. General Marshall put it differently: "It was no demobilization, it was a rout." In a speech given on September 21, 1950, the day he was sworn in

---

7   Lengthy Kennan quote in *Marshall Papers*, Vol. 7, document 79.

US soldiers fire a 105 mm howitzer gun in Korea, July 8, 1950.

as secretary of defense, he said: "Again after 1945 and 46 we demonstrated that we still had not learned our lesson despite another catastrophic world war."[8]

The United States had already withdrawn its forces from Korea, and General MacArthur could send only three divisions from Japan. These were not complete top-of-the-line units; too many of their troops had grown soft on garrison duty, and their training had been somewhat neglected. Too much of their equipment was obsolete World War II vintage. They were sent to Korea without the winter uniforms they would desperately need later. Nevertheless, MacArthur sent a report to Washington stating that "United States combat forces into the Korean battle area" were indispensable. Sole reliance on air and sea power was "a waste of time."

---

8   Halberstam, *Coldest Winter*, p. 179. *Marshall Papers*, Vol. 7, document 106.

The president did not hesitate to send American soldiers although he later wrote that he did not want to start another world war: "Must be careful not to cause a general Asiatic war." Marshall agreed completely. Both had their eyes on Europe, which they considered the key arena in the cold war. Truman later admitted that this was the most difficult decision of his presidency, even harder than deciding to use atomic weapons in August 1945.[9]

At the time, few Americans knew or cared much about the two regimes on the Korean peninsula. It also seemed that the US government was equally indifferent. As has already been noted, on January 12, 1950, Secretary of State Dean Acheson had given an extemporaneous speech to the National Press Club in which he named the vital areas for US defense in the western Pacific. His line included the island chain extending from the Alaskan Aleutians to the south and west through Japan and the Ryukyu Islands to the Philippines. He omitted both Formosa and Korea from America's defense perimeter. Congressional Republicans decried the omission of Formosa, proof that Truman and Marshall had "lost China." But there was hardly a peep in the US about the fact that Korea had been dropped. One editorialist did claim at the time that Acheson's speech was "an invitation to aggression against South Korea."[10]

While it fell on indifference in America, Acheson's remarks were noted with intense interest by North Korean leader Kim Il-sung and Soviet chief Joseph Stalin, who ultimately gave Kim the green light to attack South Korea. Historians differ about the degree to which the secretary's remarks might have helped bring about the subsequent war. His friend Averell

---

9   McCullough, *Truman*, pp. 782–83.

10   D. Clayton James with Anne Sharp Wells, *Refighting the Last War: Command and Crisis in Korea 1950–1953*, p. 134. See this for the context of Acheson's comments.

Harriman later admitted: "I am afraid Dean really blew it on that one." David Halberstam called it "a colossal gaffe." George F. Kennan wrote in his memoirs that "we are victims mainly of an absolutely unbelievable and stupendous military blunder." All that could be done after Acheson's slip-up was to "pick up the pieces."[11]

Nobody could have imagined that by 1953, warfare in that mountainous and sometimes freezing land would claim the lives of 33,651 American soldiers, three thousand UN allies, as well as roughly two and a half million Koreans and more than 180,000 Chinese. General Marshall was one of the few Americans who knew a lot about it, thanks to his almost half of a century of service that included assignments in the Philippines and China and as America's top diplomat from 1947 to 1949. As chief of staff in the final weeks of World War II, he had a hand in the important decisions dealing with the future of the Korean peninsula. Later as secretary of state, he had advocated a gradual phasing out of US troops until South Korea would control its own armed forces.[12] However, when the June 25 attack occurred, he was in retirement. Not until almost three months later, on September 21, 1950, was he sworn in as the country's third secretary of defense.

By early August 1950, the advance of the North Korean invading force was slowing down. This was due in part to their lengthening supply lines, which were increasingly stretched the

---

11   McCullough, *Truman*, p. 777. Brands, *General*, pp. 47–49. Halberstam, *Coldest Winter*, pp. 1, 48. George F. Kennan, *Memoirs, 1950–1963*, pp. 33–38, 182. For the Acheson–Marshall relationship, see Robert L. Beisner, *Dean Acheson: A Life in the Cold War*, p. 414. Acheson was unable to "challenge the sainted Marshall," "the colossal Marshall," and was "overawed" by MacArthur, whom he called the "Sorcerer of Inchon."

12   Figures from Allan R. Millett, "Korean War," *Britannica Online Encyclopedia. Marshall Papers*, Vol. 7, document 128.

farther south the invaders marched. They also became more vulnerable to air attacks. From the beginning the meager and outnumbered American forces and their southern Korean allies enjoyed air and sea supremacy over and around the southern half of the peninsula. They were pushed relentlessly toward a minuscule part of the country in the southeast—the port of Pusan, from which an evacuation could be executed if that became necessary. However, the more the Americans and South Koreans were shoved southward, the shorter, more compact and more defensible their line became. There was less ground to be defended, and the shorter supply and communication lines became more manageable. This Pusan Perimeter became an effective bulwark against the invading Communists and enabled the UN forces to gain time until help could arrive. Finally an encouraged Eighth Army commander, General Walton H. "Johnny" Walker, declared that "there will be no more retreating, withdrawal or readjustment of the lines....There is not going to be a Dunkirk or Bataan. A retreat would be one of the greatest butcheries in history. We must fight to the end."[13]

INCHON AND THE ILLUSION OF VICTORY

The overall commander of both US and UN armed forces, General Douglas MacArthur, who had been focusing on his primary duty of pacifying and modernizing Japan, decided that conditions were ideal for one of the most daring and dangerous brainchilds in his brilliant fifty-two-year military career: an attack via the port of Inchon, a short distance to the west from the occupied southern capital of Seoul. If the port were taken, UN troops could recapture Seoul, strike at the rear of the North's army, cut off its supply lines, paralyze the troops' fighting

---

13   Halberstam, *Coldest Winter*, pp. 166–67. Following MacArthur gamble quote in Hampton Sides, *On Desperate Ground: The Marines at the Reservoir, the Korean War's Greatest Battle*, pp. 9, 15.

General MacArthur and his "court" during the Inchon landing.

power, and encircle and capture them, thereby ending the war. MacArthur himself said that this attack, known officially as "Operation Chromite," was a "5,000-to-1 gamble."

US troops had gone ashore there at the end of the Second World War. But an opposed landing was something entirely different. Chief of Naval Operations Admiral Forrest Sherman noted that the port had "every conceivable geographical natural handicap." Its tides were among the world's highest, and they drained the harbor two times each day, leaving large mudflats at ebb tide that could easily trap naval vessels that did not exit early enough. There was sufficient water for landing craft only at high tide, which came only about every three weeks. In other words, if the attack had not taken place on September 15, 1950, as MacArthur planned, the daring operation could not have been launched until October 11. Because the approaches to the harbor were rocky and laden with shoals, the landing had to be made at daylight; it began at 5:30 a.m. in full view of any troops deployed on shore to mount a defense. This would make tactical surprise almost impossible. Attacking ships would have to maneuver around and capture the fortified island of Wolmi-do, located in the middle of the channel. Since there were no beaches at the port, soldiers had to scale the seawalls, which ascended a dozen feet or more from the water.[14]

A confident General MacArthur argued that precisely because of the seeming impossibility of capturing Inchon, the enemy would not deploy a large number of soldiers to defend it. He was later proved to be right. But most experts were skeptical that it was feasible. The president could not say no and ultimately came around. General Matthew B. Ridgway, who would soon assume command of all operations in Korea, was enthusiastic about the operation. The Joint Chiefs of Staff (JCS) tried unsuccessfully to talk MacArthur out of it. General Omar Bradley said "it was the wildest kind of military plan—Pattonesque."[15] They waited until a week before the attack to give their approval. Marshall had not been sworn in as defense secretary until four days later, so he had no influence on the planning or operation.

The attack involved 260 naval vessels. Due to the tide, they had only four hours to do their precise work, and they benefitted from almost complete surprise. The assault began with a forty-eight-hour bombardment by American and British ships and warplanes from Japan. There was no return fire. As was his practice eleven times during the Second World War, MacArthur rode into the thick of battle on one of the ships. To his pleasant surprise, the North Koreans had not mined the harbor, enabling the operation to proceed while suffering relatively light casualties. By the end of the day, twenty-one American soldiers were dead and one hundred seventy-four wounded.

---

14   Condit, *Test*, p. 66.

15   Halberson, *Coldest Winter*, p. 218. Brands, *General*, pp. 153–58.

The Marines and Army together formed the X Corps commanded by Virginia Military Institute (VMI) graduate General Ned Almond from Luray, Virginia. They took possession of the rugged Wolmi Island and stormed over the sea walls, quickly neutralizing the weak defenses deployed by the North. They then captured Kimpo airfield and raced to Seoul, which fell ten days later. The South Korean government was restored to power in the capital, Seoul. By September 23, the North Korean units were forced to withdraw from the Pusan Perimeter; soon they were on the run. Only twenty-five thousand to thirty thousand North Korean soldiers escaped the trap. On September 27, General Walker's troops met up with the troops who had captured Inchon. They thought the war would be over soon.

On September 30, nine days after he had been sworn in, Defense Secretary Marshall cabled the victorious MacArthur: "Accept my personal tribute to the courageous campaign you directed in Korea and the daring and perfect strategical operation, which virtually terminated the struggle." MacArthur answered: "Thanks, George, for your fine message. It brings back vividly the memories of past wars and the complete coordination and perfect unity of cooperation, which has always existed in our mutual relationship and martial endeavors." MacArthur no doubt was aware that Marshall disliked being addressed by his first name. President Truman also sent a message to MacArthur: "Well and nobly done."[16]

A stunned Omar Bradley exclaimed that "Inchon proved to be the luckiest military operation in history." "The swiftness and magnitude of the victory were mind-boggling." One week, they were dreading the prospect of a Dunkirk-style evacuation. Two

---

16 *Marshall Papers*, Vol. 7, document 111. Brands, *General*, pp. 165–166. Sides, *On Desperate Ground*, pp. 9–13. Note biographies of Almond, who commanded the operation, and the Marine major general who planned it, Oliver Prince Smith, pp. 17, 31–32, 42–43.

weeks later, they were savoring a dazzling victory. MacArthur sent the North Koreans a surrender demand on October 1, which the Kim regime quickly rejected. The allies were thus left with a difficult decision: what should they do next?[17]

When President Truman was asked in his first press conference after the sensational Inchon operation what the UN troops would do when they reached the 38th parallel, he answered that that was a decision for the UN to make. The problem was that the return of the Soviet ambassador after his boycott had made decision-making far more difficult at the UN. There was no clear indication what UN troops should do. Most did not want an occupation of the inhospitable North. MacArthur wanted to take advantage of the chaotic situation his Inchon victory had created to destroy the North Korean army. He had already ordered US warplanes to operate in North Korean airspace.

Under the confused and hurried circumstances, Truman decided to notify MacArthur that "your military objective is the destruction of the North Korean armed forces," as the JCS declared on September 27. This was sent with various important provisos. There must be no entry into North Korea of Soviet or Chinese troops. If they did appear, UN forces were to assume a defensive posture and report immediately to Washington. UN forces were not to cross the Manchurian or Soviet borders in the north. "As a matter of policy," non-Korean ground troops were not to be deployed in northern border areas. No air or naval forces were to be used against either Soviet or Manchurian territory.[18]

The JCS approved MacArthur's response the next day, September 28, for a two-prong advance against the North.

---

17   Brands, *General*, pp. 165, 169. Cray, *General*, Chapter XL, "Imperator," pp. 691–705.

18   *Marshall Papers*, Vol. 7, document 107. Condit, *Test*, p. 67. Brands, *General*, pp. 169–71.

Marshall got President Truman's and Secretary of State Acheson's approval of MacArthur's military plan. Walker's Eighth Army was to head north on the western side of the peninsula and seize the northern capital of Pyongyang. The Tenth Corps from Inchon, composed of both Marine and Army elements, was to be shipped around to the eastern port of Wonsan and was to operate separately from the Eighth Army as both move north. Such a division of forces in a mountainous land would later create near fatal problems for allied forces.[19]

The new secretary of defense added a note to the US commander in a telegram sent on September 29 and approved by President Truman. He wrote that "we want you to feel unhampered tactically and strategically to proceed north of 38th parallel." Every authority in Washington including Marshall favored crossing the parallel after such a dramatic success at Inchon had opened up the possibility of a quick victory in the war and a rapid departure from Korea. Averell Harriman said later that "it would have taken a superhuman effort to say no." "Psychologically it was almost impossible to not go ahead and complete the job." Dean Acheson, who called MacArthur "the sorcerer of Inchon," exclaimed that "there's no stopping MacArthur now."

Earlier in September, the National Security Council had drawn up NSC 81, which presented the aims for US policy in Korea: "to bring about the complete independence and unity of Korea." But it was made clear that these goals were not to be pursued by means of general war. "In no circumstances should other UN forces—particularly US forces—be used in the north-eastern province bordering the Soviet Union or in the area along the Manchurian border." Since the allies preferred not to have a vote on crossing the 38th parallel, MacArthur should simply do it if he "found it militarily necessary to do so."

---

19   Condit, *Test*, p. 67.

There were, however, three main stipulations: MacArthur's troops were not to cross either the Soviet or Manchurian borders. He was not to order American aircraft to fly over Chinese or Russian territory. Nor was he to order UN forces—as opposed to South Korean troops—to reach the Yalu River at the Korean-Chinese border. If China or the Soviet Union were to send soldiers into Korea, MacArthur was told to notify Washington immediately. MacArthur would later point to this telegram from Marshall to justify stretching his orders and sending his troops all the way to the Yalu River border to China, even though he had been forbidden to do so. MacArthur responded to Marshall's note that "unless and until the enemy capitulates I regard all of Korea open for our mil operations."[20]

No one objected to Marshall's telegram to MacArthur. Secretary of State Acheson sought an explanation for it: "To me, the message seems directed toward soothing MacArthur's irritation at being required to submit his plan of operations." Acheson was assured that Washington wanted MacArthur to feel unhampered in proceeding north, except as his orders confined

20   Brands, *General*, p. 147–48. William Manchester, *American Caesar: Douglas MacArthur 1880–1964*, pp. 71, 540, 550. John W. Spanier, *The Truman–MacArthur Controversy and the Korean War*, pp. 100–101, 123. D. Clayton James argued that Marshall's chief failure during the Korean War was his "failing to insist on closer control over MacArthur after Inchon and not having his directive revised or countermanded" after the Chinese entered the war. His message of September 29, 1950, was Marshall's most controversial mistake. It contributed to the "dissonance in the chain of command." See James' chapter in William M. Leary, ed., *MacArthur and the American Century*, pp. 394, 453. Also D. Clayton James, *The Years of MacArthur. Triumph and Disaster 1945–1964*. Acheson called Marshall's hesitancy toward MacArthur "curious quiescence." The Ungers wrote that Marshall "seemed as irresolute as the others." Unger, *Marshall*, pp. 461, 467–68. Harriman and Acheson quotes in Sides, *On Desperate Ground*, p. 52. Sides added that "in so many words MacArthur was issued a hall pass to go wherever he pleased."

him. On October 7, the UN General Assembly, in which the Soviets have no veto power, called for elections in all of Korea and the creation of a unified, independent and democratic government for all Korea. The UN coalition's goal of saving South Korea had clearly changed to the unification of Korea.[21]

Two weeks after Inchon, September 30, 1950, a South Korean division, followed on October 7 by units from the US First Cavalry Division crossed the 38th parallel on the way to capturing Pyongyang. A week later, October 7, Marshall demonstrated his role as the channel between the JCS and the president. He got approval from Truman and passed it on the JCS that if major Chinese units entered the conflict, MacArthur should continue the battle if his troops had a "reasonable chance of success." It was made clear, however, that he would have to get permission from Washington before launching attacks against Chinese territory.[22]

MARSHALL'S LEADERSHIP

MacArthur disagreed with Truman, Marshall, Acheson, and the JCS and others in the administration on many things. The most important were the need to limit the war, to desist from attacks on Chinese and Soviet territory, and to maintain the focus on Europe as the premier arena for surviving the Cold War. Marshall was a powerful voice in maintaining this consensus, but the most important decisions were made by the president.

---

21   *Marshall Papers*, Vol. 7, document 110. Condit, *Test*, pp. 67–68. Brands, *General*, pp. 170–171. McCullough, *Truman*, p. 799. Acheson, *Present*, pp. 453–54. James/Wells discuss the context within which Marshall's message should be understood. James/Wells, *Refighting*, pp. 17, 184, 198. John Toland. *In Mortal Combat: Korea 1950–1953*, pp. 250, 273, 429. Also William Stueck, *The Korean War: An International History*, pp. 114–15, 133, 175, 348–49.

22   Condit, *Test*, p. 68. Pogue, *Marshall*, p. 457. Stoler, *Marshall*, pp. 184–86.

President Truman with his chief military adviser,
Secretary of Defense George C. Marshall.

Marshall was what one scholar called "the president's deputy for military affairs."[23] He had a seat in the National Security Council, where fundamental policy was made, and he could weigh in on policy matters, including NATO. Due to his control over the defense budget, he was the arbiter of disagreements between the military services. While defense secretary, he considerably facilitated the interaction between political, diplomatic, and military actors.

During his time in office, the JCS could make recommendations to the president only through the secretary of defense unless the president invited them to do so. The chiefs did not have direct access to the president although the JCS chief met with the president about twice a week to brief him

---

23   Condit, *Test*, p. iv.

on military developments, not to pass on JCS decisions. They advised the secretary of defense who discussed their thoughts with the president. As a group they had no direct command over American fighting forces. Orders had to go through one of the three military services. US commanders in Korea reported to the Army chief, General J. Lawton "Lightning Joe" Collins.[24]

With UN troops approaching their border with North Korea and with the UN commander, General MacArthur, speaking openly of bombing inside China itself, the Chinese leadership concluded that their troops could no longer stay out of the fighting. When MacArthur's soldiers ran into a swarm of Chinese troops, who could fight very well in Korea's inhospitable terrain, Marshall consistently refused to make tactical decisions himself. Referring to the wide scattering of American forces in northern Korea, he said: "I don't know what MacArthur intends to do about that. It is his problem. I won't even ask MacArthur what he is going to do. We have no business, here in Washington, 8,000 miles away, asking the local commander what his tactical plans are....All during the Battle of the Bulge the War Department did not ask them one single question. We let them do the fighting. It's the same way now. We must follow hour by hour any developments pertaining to our getting further involved with the Chinese Communists, but we won't ask MacArthur his tactical plans."[25]

Marshall's style of leadership during his involvement in the Korean War was the same as it had been in the Second World War: carefully select the best officers available for specific jobs. Encourage them and supply them with what they need to achieve the objectives. Back them up. But allow them to decide

---

24   "Joint Chiefs of Staff," *U.S. News*, pp. 13–14.

25   Brands, *General*, pp. 215–16. For greater detail of Chinese thinking at the time, see Halberstam, *Coldest Winter*, pp. 354–56, and Sides, *On Desperate Ground*, pp. 66–68.

the military means for achieving those goals. Never attempt to impose your own will on the commander in the faraway field.

David Halberstam was an admiring critic of Marshall. He called him "the most respected public official of the era." "Of the senior group, he was the most knowledgeable and experienced, an icon of icons, more like a father figure than a peer to most of the men serving Truman. He was the quietest and most modest great figure of an era: he never raised his voice, never gave angry commands, never threatened or bullied people. His strength came from his sense of purpose and duty, which were absolute; his almost unique control of his ego; and his ability to separate what mattered from what did not." Halberstam went on to mention Marshall's "intellectual firepower." It was "the most pragmatic kind of intelligence, never flashy." At the same time, he wondered why the secretary was so "passive" in not restraining MacArthur when he made dangerous decisions. Halberstam applied the same criticism to the JCS and Secretary of State Dean Acheson.[26] It would have violated Marshall's fundamental leadership practices to have tried to make the tactical decisions for MacArthur.

WAKE ISLAND SUMMIT

Truman had been in the White House five and one-half years and had never met MacArthur. Twice he had asked the general to return to the US for talks, but the latter begged off both times. This time Truman asked Marshall what he thought about a visit with MacArthur. Marshall supported it. But in light of the congressional elections in a couple of weeks, he did not think it would be a good idea to meet in the politicized national capital. Marshall sent a message to MacArthur expressing the president's wish and recommended a meeting in Honolulu. If that were too far, given his wartime command requirements, they could meet at Wake Island in the western Pacific.

---

26   Halberstam, *Coldest Winter*, pp. 480–82.

Wake Island is located seven thousand miles from Washington and two thousand miles from MacArthur's headquarters in Tokyo. It was a three-day trip for the president and a sixteen-hour roundtrip for the general. A diminutive atoll in the middle of the Pacific Ocean, just west of the international dateline, it offered a number of rusting Quonset huts erected by Pan American Airways. Over the years, shipwrecked sailors, castaways, merchants, and whalers found refuge on this once uninhabited island. It had been the scene of bitter fighting during the Second World War. Being the only terrain within a thousand miles that could accommodate an airstrip, it has served as a mid-oceanic refueling stop for the far-flung American presence in Asia.

The general was not happy about this and suspected that deep down the president wanted to bask in the victorious glow of Inchon so close to the midterm election date. All agreed to meet at Wake Island on Sunday, October 15. In the end only General Bradley accompanied the president. Not wishing to mix politics with policy, Marshall and Acheson remained in Washington to meet two visiting French ministers. This was regrettable since the state and defense secretaries were the two men who could have questioned MacArthur and his plans in a more detailed and effective way.[27] As it was, the talks were more superficial than they should have been. The agenda called for discussions of Korea in the morning; lunch; discussions in the afternoon on Japan, Philippines, and other hot spots in Asia without staffs; dinner; and a press release afterwards.

Truman wanted to get the measure of MacArthur and possibly test the accuracy of his private nicknames for him: "Play actor and bunco man," "Mr. Prima Donna Brass Hat," and

---

27   *Marshall Papers*, Vol. 7, document 124. See Acheson, *Present*, pp. 456–57. Halberstam, *Coldest Winter*, pp. 368–70. Unger, *Marshall*, p. 466. Sides, *On Desperate Ground*, pp. 56–61.

"supreme egotist." He said when he left Washington that he was going to "have a talk with God's right hand man."[28] He wanted more importantly to inform himself of the course of the war in Korea. He wanted to make sure that the general understood that the fighting there must remain limited and should under no circumstances be widened to include Chinese or Soviet troops.

The summit got off to a bad start when MacArthur did not salute the commander-in-chief upon arrival. This display of disrespect was a shocking violation of long-standing protocol. Truman was also put off that the general wore an open-collar shirt and his legendary tattered hat to this meeting with his boss. However, MacArthur was courteous and asked the president if he could smoke. Truman answered in the affirmative and added: "I suppose I've had more smoke blown in my face than any other man alive."[29] MacArthur apologized for the embarrassment his critical message to the Veterans of Foreign Wars a few weeks earlier had caused the president. It had questioned the administration's policy in Korea. More such public critiques of his country's policies would follow.

Truman thought the talks went very well. What the general did not know was that a stenographer, Vernice Anderson, whom Marine MPs had forbidden to take a walk along the beach during the talks, was consigned to a chair right outside the meeting room. With nothing else to do, she recorded every word the leaders spoke. This protocol recorded the assurances MacArthur had given to the president. It was an embarrassment to MacArthur later during his congressional hearing following his dismissal.

MacArthur presented an entirely optimistic picture of the fortunes of war in Korea: It was very unlikely the Chinese would

28 McCullough, *Truman*, p. 793. Brands, *General*, p. 176. Sides, *On Desperate Ground*, p. 59.

29 Brands, *General*, p. 177.

intervene. If they did, they would suffer the "greatest slaughter in the history of mankind." Nor would the Russians intervene; they lacked the needed ground troops. Organized resistance would be finished by Thanksgiving. The one hundred thousand Communist Korean soldiers in the North were stubborn but inferior and poorly equipped. Since the war was nearly over, he hoped the Eighth Army would be withdrawn to Japan by Christmas. Two divisions and the UN troops would remain on the peninsula until elections could be held. Other American troops and their equipment could be sent to Europe. Finally the Japanese were ready for a peace treaty.[30]

Truman was elated by this positive report. He exclaimed: "No one who was not here would believe we have covered so much ground." "This has been a most satisfactory conference." However, it ended unsatisfactorily. MacArthur asked the president: "If it's all right, I am anxious to get back as soon as possible and would like to leave before luncheon, if that is convenient." Although presented in a courteous way, it was unacceptable for a subordinate to depart before the commander-in-chief had ended the session. Truman awarded the general a fifth oak leaf cluster for his Distinguished Service Medal and shook the hand of his departing commander, whose Inchon halo would disappear in only a couple of weeks. The Chinese had begun to move south even before he had boarded his plane.[31]

INTO THE TRAP

The vehicle-bound American and South Korean troops moved rapidly northward meeting only scattered resistance. They captured the northern capital of Pyongyang on October 20. This was the first time a communist capital had been captured and freed since the onset of the Cold War. Two groups of UN

30   Brands, *General*, pp. 179–84. Condit, *Test*, p. 69.

31   Brands, *General*, pp. 182–83.

forces proceeded north on two separate sides of the peninsula, and troops were scattered thinly over the mountainous terrain on the assumption that the Chinese would not intervene. Of all the doctrines of the American military, not splitting commands was among the most sacred. Acheson worried about this, but he considered himself too much of a military amateur to question the top generals. Both Marshall and Bradley explained that the JCS could not command troops seven thousand miles away. But Acheson suspected that both were in awe of "the MacArthur mystique" after the stunning against-all-odds success at Inchon. In a long-shot gamble, he would somehow win, they thought. After the fall of Pyongyang, many people thought the war was, in effect, already over.[32]

Compounding the UN's problems were serious intelligence breakdowns. Author Hampton Sides described this problem as "one of the most egregious intelligence failures in American military history." No fewer than twenty-seven Chinese divisions containing 250,000 to 300,000 Chinese soldiers, many of whom battle-hardened from the recent Chinese civil war, were ready and waiting on their side of the Yalu River. MacArthur and his staff grossly underestimated the enemy's numbers and fighting ability. General Almond admonished his troops: "Don't let a bunch of goddamn Chinese laundrymen stop you!" The recently created CIA also believed it unlikely that Chinese soldiers would fight in Korea. Covert assistance to North Koreans was considered more likely.[33]

---

32   Halberstam, *Coldest Winter*, pp. 314–15. Acheson, *Present*, p. 466–67.

33   Halberstam, *Coldest Winter*, p. 314. Brands, *General*, p. 194. Sides, *On Desperate Ground*, pp. 89, 99, 132–33, 198–99. See Sides, *On Desperate Ground*, for all aspects of the plan to divide the UN forces and the disastrous First Marine Division advance up the snowy mountainous eastern part of the Korean Peninsula to the Chosin Reservoir within a few miles from the Chinese border, where a Chinese trap awaited them, written in gripping style in which the reader can feel the minus

Diplomatic signals were also missed by the allies. The US had no diplomatic relations with the newly created People's Republic of China (PRC), so top Chinese officials sent signals to the Americans through India's ambassador to China, K.M. Panikkar. When the first message was ignored—that the PRC would respond if the Americans crossed into North Korea—a second was sent by Foreign Minister Chou-En-lai on October 1, 1950, the first anniversary of the founding the PRC: if the Americans entered North Korea, the Chinese would resist. South Korean troops would be tolerated. American leaders did not trust Panikkar, in part because Nehru's India was socialist at the time and friendly to China's Communists. They considered the warnings to be bluffs and disregarded them. The consequences were terrible.[34]

MacArthur ordered his troops to advance to the northern Korean border. Since they were to advance quickly, they were only equipped lightly, depending on airdrops for limited supplies. On October 25, Chinese soldiers appeared out of nowhere to confront the shocked American troops, who had heard rumors that they would be going home soon. Their South Korean and UN allies were also overwhelmed. The Chinese wanted to slow the Americans' and Koreans' advance and to test their combat abilities. In the single battle at Onjong-Unsan,

---

twenty–degree temperatures. He describes this as "one of the most heroic and harrowing operations in American military history, and one of the classic battles of all time." Twenty thousand vastly outnumbered Americans fought ferociously and courageously to escape the trap that had been set for them.

34   Brands, *General*, p. 194. Condit, *Test*, p. 72. During his mission to China, Marshall had learned to respect Chou–En–lai: "I found him to be one of the ablest negotiators with whom I had come in contact. He was very agreeable, clever and inscrutable in the sense that one could never quite tell what his objectives were or intentions of the moment." *Marshall Papers*, Vol. 7, document 302.

many UN troops were surrounded, and seven South Korean and American regiments were decimated. UN forces suffered over a thousand casualties at Unsan, demonstrating that the Chinese were unmistakably committed to the fighting. One military spokesman described what took place as "a massacre Indian-style, like the one that hit Custer at the Little Big Horn." The Americans had no alternative than to run for their lives, and many were captured.[35]

Although the Chinese suffered ten thousand casualties, they confirmed their successful battle tactics against the UN soldiers: attack only at night, move quickly and right through the enemy lines to sow panic and confusion in the enemy ranks, sever supply and withdrawal routes, set traps and ambush enemy forces that are counterattacking, stay off the roads, and make the most of cover and concealment.

The stunned UN troops faced bothersome hardships. Winter was approaching, and they were still in summer uniforms. They waited and waited for winter clothing. When it finally arrived, it was unable to protect the soldiers from this kind of cruel bitter cold. The freezing weather became the "third combatant."

Their World War II equipment was obsolete, and there was never enough ammunition. Supply lines became too stretched. It was ideal guerrilla country. Fending off nocturnal charges, one often did not know where the attackers were and how many of them were ready to come at you. They were literally in the dark about the status of their flanks, and they regarded South Korean units as poorly motivated and unreliable. Allied soldiers were largely mechanized and restricted to roads, which in reality were all too often nothing more than dirt tracks.

Chinese soldiers on foot could more easily move through the woods and seize the high ground. Lacking more advanced

---

35   Halberstam, *Coldest Winter*, pp. 24, 42, 198–99. Sides, *On Desperate Ground*, p. 101.

communications gear, the Chinese signaled their movement by means of bugles and other musical instruments. In the middle of the night, these sounds terrified GIs and their co-combatants. Marshall especially respected the enemy's ability to move quickly and surreptitiously in such hostile mountainous terrain.[36]

The allies had to confront an additional danger: the appearance of MIG-15 jet fighters over North Korea flown by Soviet pilots and bearing Korean and Chinese markings. This sparked a competition lasting more than two years over control of the air. Ultimately America's F-86 Saber jet interceptors gained the upper hand and conducted offensive air attacks all over North Korea that offered some protection for UN troops and B-29 bombers. But the MIGs deployed from China and operating in "MIG alley" presented a daunting barrier to allied pilots flying on or near the Yalu River.[37]

The allies lost about eight thousand men in this first of five Chinese offensives, six thousand of whom were South Korean. They were forced to pull back and tighten their supply lines. And then, as suddenly as they came, the Chinese simply disappeared on November 6, 1950, after only eleven days in battle.[38] In retrospect it becomes clear that this was MacArthur's last opportunity to avoid the disaster that was to come by ordering his troops to withdraw to a line by Pyongyang or the 38th parallel. But the commander was intent on a victory that would leave a unified Korea, even if that meant bombing the bridges over the Yalu and, if necessary, bombing across that river to destroy Chinese military and industrial targets. Marshall, the JCS and

---

36   See Halberstam, *Coldest Winter*, pp. 16–21. Sides, *On Desperate Ground*, pp. 113–15. For Chinese methods of fighting, see pp. 66–68, 97–98, 135–39.

37   Millett, "Korean War." Sides, *On Desperate Ground*, pp. 106–7.

38   Sides, *On Desperate Ground*, pp. 106–7.

the Truman administration were just as determined to limit the fighting to the Korean peninsula.

On November 7, 1950, the day MacArthur ordered bombing north of his troops' lines, Marshall sent MacArthur a telegram saying that "We all realize your difficulty in fighting a desperate battle in a mountainous region under winter conditions and with a multi-national force in all degrees of military preparedness. I also understand, I think, the difficulty involved in conducting such a battle under necessarily limited conditions....However this appears to be unavoidable but I want you to know that I understand your problem....We are faced with an extremely grave international problem which could easily lead to a world disaster."[39]

One thing Marshall did not understand was MacArthur's warning that the morale of his troops would be threatened if they were not explained for what they are risking their lives. Acheson recalls that Marshall told then Colonel Dean Rusk "that when a general complains of the morale of his troops, the time has come to look into his own." He would note later that "we were at our lowest point" at that time.[40]

For MacArthur retreat would be tantamount to appeasement. Although the situation of his army was dire, he was sure that he could end the war with victory. His proclamation on November 24, 1950, was full of optimism: "If successful, this should for all practical purposes end the war, restore peace and unity to Korea." What was needed at this point was nothing more than a mopping-up operation.[41]

Marshall supported this offensive. Both he and Acheson expressed the opinion in a November 21 meeting that

39   *Marshall Papers*, Vol. 7, pp. 226–29 and document 148.

40   *Marshall Papers*, Vol. 7, pp. 323–24.

41   Brands, *General*, p. 212.

"MacArthur should push forward with the planned offensive." On that same day, elements of the Seventh Regiment of the Seventh Division arrived at the Yalu River in violation of the restriction that only South Korean troops were permitted to operate near the borders with China and the Soviet Union. The unit's senior officers were reported to have celebrated by urinating in the river. However, the defense secretary did react to the commander's misguided "home by Christmas" statement made to the president at the Wake Island summit. In Marshall's opinion, it was "an embarrassment which we must get around in some manner."[42]

Within 24 hours, the UN troops ran into a mighty wall of 420,000 Chinese and North Korean regulars in the West. MacArthur had said that there could not be more than thirty thousand Chinese troops in the area; "otherwise my intelligence would know about it." The commander had sent the Eighth Army into the biggest ambush in US military history and necessitated the longest retreat in America's past. He had also ordered General Almond's Tenth Corps to move north on the eastern side of the peninsula despite the better judgment of the general commanding the Marine First Division within that force, Major General O.P. Smith. Colliding with two Chinese armies, the Marines were surrounded near the Chosin Reservoir and were forced to "advance to the rear" by fighting and stumbling southward through the worst sub-zero winter weather imaginable. One journalist wrote: "Most of the Marines were so numb and exhausted that they didn't even bother to take cover at sporadic machine-gun and rifle fire." Nevertheless, they destroyed seven Chinese divisions along the way before reaching their base camp at Hungnam on December 11. President Truman remembered that Marshall "appeared fairly certain" that the Eighth Army would hold its ground, and

---

42   *Marshall Papers*, Vol. 7, pp. 259, 261. Halberstam, *Coldest Winter*, p. 390. Sides, *On Desperate Ground*, pp. 124–25.

that Tenth Corps would succeed in extracting itself from the dangerous trap into which it had stumbled.[43]

The shock in America of this rude reversal, so soon after MacArthur's "home by Christmas" promise, was enormous. Acheson remembered that "we sat around like paralyzed rabbits while MacArthur carried out this nightmare."[44] MacArthur exclaimed that "we face an entirely new war" as he went on the defensive. He demanded an end to restraints on his authority to bomb Chinese facilities along the Yalu. Washington resisted. Nevertheless, Truman asserted that "we cannot afford to damage MacArthur's prestige at this point. Marshall tried to reassure his colleagues. He admitted that the situation was "very critical," but he called on them to be "very calm and very careful and very wise in forming our conclusions....The intense desire of all is to proceed in such a way that we can avoid a full world war." He emphasized that "we should not get into war with the Chinese Communists."[45]

Marshall called the war with China "a gigantic booby trap."[46] "How can we get out with honor?" This was a question he asked often. In a meeting on December 2, he said "that we were in a great dilemma of determining how we could save our troops and protect our national honor at the same time." He found it difficult to abandon the South Korean allies. He argued that the UN forces could not abandon Korea "in good conscience."[47] Marshall

43   Brands, *General*, pp. 212, 238–39. Truman, *Years of Trial*, pp. 419, 421–22. Unger, *Marshall*, pp. 463–64, 468. Sides, *On Desperate Ground*, pp. 118, 192–93.

44   Halberstam, *Coldest Winter*, p. 44. Acheson, *Present*, pp. 469–71.

45   *Marshall Papers*, Vol. 7, pp. 226–27, 259–61 and document 165. Unger, *Marshall*, p. 468.

46   McCullough, *Truman*, pp. 815–17.

47   *Marshall Papers*, Vol. 7, document 173. Pogue, *Marshall*, p. 466.

exclaimed that "we must not dig ourselves into a hole without an exit."[48] He never wavered from his conviction that the Cold War would be won or lost in Europe and that the Soviet Union, not China, was the principal enemy. President Truman agreed whole heartedly. Korea had a certain symbolic significance, but it was not strategically vital.[49] George F. Kennan met with Marshall in December 1950 and found him to be a "calm, wise and steady ally," who favored gaining time in the war and "hanging on doggedly for reasons of prestige and morale."[50]

Marshall did attempt to provide some positive military spin on MacArthur's predicament. He defended the commander's decision to launch an attack that was "necessary in order to find out what the Communists were up to. Now we know."[51] This statement shows how far Marshall was willing to go to stick up for a fellow five-star general who had gotten himself and his army into deep trouble.

The First Marine Division sliced through seven Chinese divisions and components of three others. Chinese forces in the Chosin Campaign were rendered ineffective as a fighting force. They suffered astonishing casualties: 30,000 killed in action and over 12,500 wounded compared with 750 US Marines killed, 3,000 wounded and fewer than 200 missing. Nevertheless, both sides proclaimed victory. MacArthur described the withdrawal as a success. The Marines' ability to elude a frigid trap in an unforgiving mountainous area was a shot in the arm for the home front, which had heard too much depressing news of the war. On December 18, 1950, *Time* described it as "a battle unparalleled in US military history." The president called it "one of the greatest

---

48   Acheson, *Present*, pp. 475–77.

49   Brands, *General*, pp. 217–19.

50   Kennan, *Memoirs*, pp. 32–38.

51   *Marshall Papers*, Vol. 7, p. 261. Sides, *On Desperate Ground*, pp. 326–27.

fighting retreats that ever was." An impressive 900,000 Marines from X Corps were evacuated by sea, and their ships also carried 100,000 North Korean refugees to the South.

To the west General Walker ordered his Eighth Army to move south. Those who were involved called this mass desperate evacuation "the big bugout." They destroyed all the equipment they could not carry and headed as fast as possible to Seoul, thereby saving the army. On December 23, Walker was killed in a car accident north of Seoul. He was on his way to present a unit citation to the Twenty-fourth Division, in which his son, Captain Samuel S. Walker, was serving. He was the highest-ranking officer to die in Korea. Only one day earlier, Marshall had written to Walker that "you are facing a very hard Christmas." "You have done a magnificent job."[52] MacArthur ordered Captain Walker to escort his father back to the United States for burial. General Walker was replaced as Eighth Army commander by the deputy army chief of staff, Lieutenant General Matthew B. Ridgway, a fighting officer of World War II fame whom Marshall admired. Ultimately, he would take over all of MacArthur's commands.[53]

On December 27, 1950, the JCS dispatched a message to MacArthur rejecting his demands for an expanded war and the dropping of atomic weapons on Beijing and other Chinese cities. The wording was unmistakable: "Korea is not the place to fight a major war….We should not commit our remaining available ground forces to action against Chinese Communist forces in Korea in face of the increased threat of a general war." MacArthur

---

52 *Marshall Papers*, Vol. 7, document 191. Sam Walker would become a four-star general and later superintendent of Marshall's alma mater, the Virginia Military Institute.

53 Matthew B. Ridgway, *The Korean War*, p. 142. General Walker could not accept MacArthur's idea of establishing enclaves in the war-torn north. For Marines' escape in the East, see Sides, *On Desperate Ground*, pp. 327–33.

was reminded of the "continuing primary mission of defense of Japan for which only troops of the Eighth Army are available." MacArthur angrily rejected the administration's Europe-first strategy. He demanded an expansion of the war to include a blockade of the China coast, air and naval bombardment to destroy China's war-making capabilities, deployment of Chinese Nationalist forces in Korea, and a diversionary operation by Chiang's army against the mainland of China. Marshall and Truman turned all of these down.[54]

Two days later, on New Year's Eve, December 31, the Chinese launched their third major assault in Korea. Before it came to an end on January 5, 1951, wide swaths of American occupied territory in the north and the southern capital of Seoul had been lost. The attackers targeted primarily South Korean units, which were displaying signs of defeatism.

NEW COMMAND IN KOREA

General Ridgway had been given a mere twenty-four-hour notice that he would be assuming command of the demoralized and retreating Eighth Army. His first stop was Tokyo to receive the command from MacArthur. Responding to Ridgway's query whether he could order the Eighth to attack the enemy, MacArthur simply said: "The Eighth Army is yours, Matt. Do what you think best."

In his inspection of his new troops, Ridgway observed that his soldiers had lost their confidence and aggressive spirit. They were not patrolling and therefore had an insufficient knowledge of where the enemy was and what its strength was. They were further thrown off balance by the December 31 attack, and they had to abandon their positions and race southward. They could not defend Seoul and had to abandon it. Trying to escape an unpleasant repeat of Communist rule, the population rushed for

---

54 *Marshall Papers*, Vol. 7, pp. 316–17, 323.

the bridges by the tens of thousands in order to beat the army out of the city.

Ridgway occupied a more solid and defensible line south of the Han and the 38th parallel. His soldiers, with their restored morale, were now able to parry the blows delivered by the Chinese. The crisis and the possibility of evacuation in defeat were now largely over. On February 27, 1951, Marshall sent Ridgway a congratulatory message telling him: "I think you are doing a magnificent job amidst many hardships...a job being well done."[55]

By the end of January 1951, Ridgway had been able to halt the third Chinese assault and to launch successful, limited counteroffensives. Generals Collins and Vandenberg visited Korea and gave high marks to the restored morale of the soldiers and the improved military situation Ridgway had brought about. There was no more talk of withdrawing from the peninsula. The UN alliance was now able, in Marshall's words, "to penalize the Chinese Communists for their aggression" in a manner that would "lead to the subversion and depletion of their military strength."[56] The UN troops aimed to inflict as many losses on the enemy as possible in order to soften China in expectation of peace talks.

In a meeting with the New Zealand prime minister on February 9, 1951, Marshall expressed his opinion that "the situation in Korea was greatly encouraging." There were problems: South Korean troops still feared the Chinese, but it helped that their units were interspersed with US and other non-Korean units. The US had to deal with a very difficult problem of replacements since units in America were being ripped apart

---

55   Brands, *General*, p. 257, 260–63. *Marshall Papers*, Vol. 7, document 248.

56   *Marshall Papers*, Vol. 7, document 223. Roy E. Appleman, *Ridgway Duels for Korea*, pp. 143–44, 406, 430–33.

to provide the needed reinforcements. The air war over Korea was improving, and attacks in the enemy homeland would be necessary only in the event of massive air attacks against allied forces.

Marshall was concerned about the defense of Japan since there was no garrison at the time. The island of Hokkaido and elsewhere was "wide open to attack." Security was being maintained by seventy-five thousand Japanese police. The island nation depended on the Eighth Army for its defense.[57]

On February 11, 1951, the Chinese attempted yet again to end the UN troops' presence on the peninsula. This was their fourth try. Their failure to win major battles at Chipyong-ni and Wonju signaled a turning point in the war: the strategic initiative shifted to the UN forces commanded by Ridgway. Although it was aimed primarily at South Korean units, the attack hit the allies forcefully enough to push them back temporarily. However, the Eighth Army recovered its balance when Ridgway's troops counterattacked on February 21 and compelled the Chinese to retreat north of the Han River in central Korea. Marshall favored remaining open on the subject of whether to continue beyond the 38th parallel. He did agree that the US should abide by any UN decisions regarding Korea.[58]

After two months of heavy fighting, UN troops again crossed the 38th parallel. The Chinese followed quickly with their fifth major assault on April 22. That was a month in which all eyes in Washington were cast on the fate of General MacArthur, whose public criticism of the president's policy in Korea led to his removal from all four of his commands on April 11, 1951.[59]

---

57   *Marshall Papers*, Vol. 7, document 233. Truman, *Years of Trial*, p. 421.

58   *Marshall Papers*, Vol. 7, pp. 407–8.

59   Millett, "Korean War."

Generals Douglas MacArthur and Matthew B. Ridgway in Korea. On April 11, 1951, MacArthur was removed from all of his four commands, which were transferred to Ridgway.

CHAPTER SIX

Old Soldiers Fade Away: MacArthur's Dismissal and Marshall's Retirement

EVEN BEFORE MARSHALL HAD ASSUMED THE OFFICE OF DEFENSE secretary on September 21, 1950, President Truman knew he had a problem with the legendary Douglas MacArthur, whom he privately called "Mr. Prima Donna, Brass Hat." He was a "supreme ego" who considered himself "something of a god." In the lead-up to MacArthur's dismissal, the most respected Republican thinker on foreign policy and State Department consultant, John Foster Dulles, met with MacArthur several times in Tokyo. After returning to the US he advised the president to retire the seventy-year-old general before he caused Truman even more trouble. The president was not taken by surprise. But he confided to Dulles that such an act was far easier said than done. There would be political hell to pay for sacking a soldier with his "heroic standing."[1]

President Truman did not have to wait long to confirm that the famous general, who had twice been a Republican candidate for the presidency in 1944 and 1948, was politically independent-

---

1   McCullough, *Truman*, p. 793.

minded. In the 1948 election he had opposed Truman, who considered it unbecoming of an active-duty officer to challenge the commander-in-chief in an election. However, he let it go because he believed MacArthur was too politically inept to be a real threat. Nevertheless the problems created by a politically ambitious supreme commander were well known to Marshall. In a letter written to General Dwight D. Eisenhower on March 6, 1945, he admitted that "making war in a democracy is not a bed of roses."[2]

A few weeks after the Korean War had begun, the Veterans of Foreign Wars (VFW) invited the general to send a message to be read at their annual meeting. MacArthur relished the opportunity. He wrote that America could employ its air power to dominate every Asian port. He painted a picture of American hegemony over the entire Pacific region, including Formosa. President Truman was trying not to use the diplomatically sensitive island to provoke China by implying that it was a protectorate of the US. He was attempting to separate America's policy toward Formosa and Korea.

MacArthur praised Truman for his decision to defend Korea, but he neglected to send the president a copy of the address, while leaking it to the VFW and numerous news organizations. It was too late to retrieve them. The timing seemed to have been intentional in that any attempt to suppress the address would be futile. Secretary of State Dean Acheson remembered never having seen the president so furious. A general has no right to make such grandiose diplomatic statements. The president insisted that major statements on the country's foreign policy originate in the White House. Truman claimed in his memoirs: "That's the day I should have fired him." He also remembered that "after that day, I knew it was only a matter of time before there'd be a showdown."[3]

---

2   Brands, *General*, p. 40. *Words of George C. Marshall*, p. 164.

3   Brands, *General*, pp. 132–37, 143, 177–78.

At his October 15, 1950, meeting on Wake Island, MacArthur had apologized for any embarrassment his address might have caused the president. Truman stretched the truth by saying that he considered the issue to be closed. It was not. In December 1950, when Chinese troops had lured UN forces into a monstrous trap, MacArthur granted an un-cleared interview to *US News & World Report*. He contended that the ensuing fighting against Chinese troops had actually brought about a positive outcome by surprising the Chinese enemy and ruining their plans. He said that all major military operations are reported and approved in advance and that the situation on the ground is not hopeless. Not surprisingly he complained about the limitations that bore down on him and his army, calling them "an enormous handicap without precedent in military history." This infuriated the president yet again. He exclaimed: "If his advice had been taken, then or later, and if we had gone ahead and bombed the Manchurian bases, we would have been openly at war with Red China and, not improbably, with Russia. World War III might very well have been upon us."[4]

By that time, the president had lost all patience with MacArthur's public complaints about the limitations he had imposed on the general. They dealt with such things as what targets could be bombed along the Chinese border and in sanctuaries within Manchuria, how closely non-Korean UN troops could approach that border, whether the Chinese coast could be blockaded, and whether troops from Formosa could be used in the Korean conflict.

On December 5/6, Truman directed Marshall and Acheson to announce that all public statements by government officials having to do with foreign or military policies must be cleared in advance by the State or Defense Department and that advance

---

4   Brands, *General*, pp. 229–33.

copies must be sent to the White House. This regulation also applied to all communications with US media, including newspapers and magazines. As with all instructions from Washington, MacArthur regarded these guidelines as mere suggestions, not direct orders. He violated them repeatedly. Again Truman wrote later: "I should have relieved [him] then and there."[5]

The hesitancy of the JCS to send clear orders to MacArthur was demonstrated by General Ridgway. He was General Collins's deputy on the JCS before being assigned to Korea in late December 1950 to assume command of the Eighth Army. Known as a no-nonsense officer, he was irritated by the chiefs' pussy-footing around the supreme commander in Korea, whose army was in full retreat. He grumbled that they seemed "in an almost superstitious awe of this larger-than-life military figure who so often had been right when everyone else had been wrong." From the beginning MacArthur's drive to the north had made him nervous. He was disappointed that MacArthur could not get the deteriorating situation under control. During a lengthy December 3 meeting, which Marshall attended, Ridgway spoke up. He argued that they had wasted too much time debating the woeful situation in Korea, but were unable to decide on action that would prevent it from going from "bad to disastrous." When he ended his statement, no one, including Marshall, said a word.

After the gathering had adjourned, he asked Air Force Chief of Staff Hoyt Vandenberg: "Why don't the chiefs send orders to MacArthur and tell him what to do?" Vandenberg merely shook his head and said: "What good would that do? He wouldn't obey the orders. What can we do?" Ridgway retorted:

---

5   *Marshall Papers*, Vol. 7, pp. 282–83. Acheson, *Present*, pp. 472–73. Truman, *Years of Trial*, pp. 377–78. The date December 5/6 reflects the time difference in Washington and Tokyo.

"You can relieve any commander who won't obey orders, can't you?" Vandenberg assumed a puzzled and amazed expression and simply walked away.[6]

SEARCH FOR A CEASE FIRE

By February 1951, the turn-around on the battlefield had made it clear that the UN troops could not be driven out of Korea unless China made an all-out effort to push them out. At the same time it became obvious that China was not committed to the kind of total war that would be required to win the conflict in the entire peninsula. Seoul had been recaptured by mid-March, and Ridgway was on the brink of driving the Chinese northward across the 38th parallel. This favorable turn of the war's fortunes created the prospect for the Truman administration to offer the enemy armistice negotiations ultimately leading to a peace settlement. The president jumped at the opportunity.

On March 20, 1951, the Joint Chiefs cabled MacArthur that the State Department, in conversation with Marshall and the JCS, was working on a presidential announcement saying that "with clearing of bulk of South Korea of aggression, United Nations now prepared to discuss conditions of settlement in Korea." MacArthur was told that "strong UN feeling persists that further diplomatic effort towards settlement should be made before any advance with major forces north of 38th parallel." Those were strong words that UN troops should remain where they were and not to take any offensive action. The general rejected any thought of a cease fire, cabling back: "Recommend that no further military restrictions be imposed upon the United Nations Command in Korea," especially the ban on attacking

---

6   Brands, *General*, pp. 236–37. Halberstam, *Coldest Winter*, pp. 482–83. Marshall had frequently told his staff not to debate problems but to solve them.

the Chinese "sanctuary" in Manchuria.[7]

On February 13, March 7, and March 15, MacArthur violated the president's December 5/6 requirement to clear all public statements in advance. His worst transgression occurred on March 24, the eve of the administration's announcement of peace terms. He undermined Truman's plan to enter peace talks by calling for his own unpromising plan without the president's permission. In a taunting and denigrating tone that no proud nation could accept, he belittled China's "exaggerated and vaunted military power" and declared that "the enemy's human wave tactics definitely failed him as our own forces become seasoned in this form of warfare....He is showing less stamina than our own troops under rigors of climate, terrain, and battle."

More important, "Red China" lacked the requisite industrial capacity, manufacturing bases, and raw materials needed for modern warfare. "The resulting disparity is such that it cannot be overcome by bravery, however fanatical, or the most gross indifference to human loss." Thus China must cease its aggression, or something far worse would happen to it: military collapse as a consequence of UN military action in its coastal areas and interior bases. He called for an end of hostilities and said he would meet in the field with the enemy's commander-in-chief to discuss terms for realizing the UN's political objectives.[8]

Truman was furious but calm as a result of this "ultimatum" and "open defiance" of his orders. Weeks of diplomatic work had been nullified. It "left me no choice—I could no longer tolerate his insubordination."[9]

---

7   *Marshall Papers*, Vol. 7, p. 459. Brands, *General*, pp. 284–86. Truman, *Years of Trial*, pp. 377–78, 418.

8   Brands, *General*, p. 286. James F. Schnabel, *Policy and Direction: The First Year*, pp. 374–77.

9   *Marshall Papers*, Vol. 7, p. 460. Acheson, *Present*, pp. 518–19. Truman,

The last straw in MacArthur's fall from power had been his positive response to a foreign policy speech delivered on February 12, 1951, by Joseph W. Martin, House minority leader. The opposition leader said "it is the great tragedy of our day that in a period of crisis we have an administration in Washington which is so bankrupt in leadership." The Korean War was merely the latest example of Democratic incompetence. Martin criticized Truman's refusal to use Chinese Nationalists in the fighting. However, the root of the problem lay in the president's obsession with Europe, which "virtually ignores the focal point of our trouble today—Asia. "What are we in Korea for, to win or to lose?" He cited MacArthur frequently and sent a copy to the general.

Such a speech by an opposition politician is not in itself remarkable. What made it so relevant in the highly politicized national capital was that MacArthur not only read and approved its contents, but he responded on May 20 with a letter to Martin. He wrote that he had submitted to the administration his views and recommendations in "most complete detail." He had advocated meeting force with maximum counterforce, not the limited warfare upon which Truman and Marshall insisted. He advocated using Chinese Nationalist troops in Korea.

He continued with a slam against the president's and the defense secretary's Europe-first policy: "It seems strangely difficult for some to realize that here in Asia is where Communist conspirators have elected to make their play for global conquest… that here we fight Europe's war with arms while the diplomats there still fight it with words; that if we lose the war to communism in Asia, the fall of Europe is inevitable; win it and Europe most

---

Years of Trial, pp. 441–44. See Billy C. Mossman, *Ebb and Flow: November 1950–July 1951*, pp. 362–65, 495. For rotation policy that began April 22, 1951, see p. 365. Also Stanley Sandler, *The Korean War: No Victors, No Vanquished*, pp. 136–39.

probably would avoid war and yet preserve freedom." He ended with his most quotable statement: "We must win. There is no substitute for victory."[10]

On April 5, Martin read the general's letter on the floor of the House and into the public record. The next day the noose tightened. Truman wrote in his diary: "This looks like the last straw. Rank insubordination. I've come to the conclusion that our Big General in the Far East must be recalled."[11]

MACARTHUR'S LAST DAYS IN COMMAND

A flurry of meetings began the next day, April 6, 1951. Marshall's overall role was to be the coordinator between the president and the JCS, obtaining a clear recommendation from the chiefs and providing the president with the information and recommendations he needed to make his decision. There is no doubt that Truman especially valued the opinions of Marshall, whom he called "the great one."[12] The president claimed later that he had reached his conclusion two weeks earlier, but that he

---

10   Brands, *General*, pp. 280–83. Acheson, *Present*, pp. 519–20. See Acheson, *Present*, chapter 54, for details of MacArthur's removal. For the administration's Europe-first policy, see James/Wells, *Refighting*, pp. 1–2, 18–19.

11   Halberstam, *Coldest Winter*, p. 602. The editors of Vol. 7 of *Marshall Papers* warn that Truman's notations in his memoirs five or more years after the fact were in some cases not exactly as he remembered them. Nevertheless, they are important general observations of his thoughts and statements at the time. See pp. 478–80. See also Brands, *General*, pp. 296–300, and Halberstam, *Coldest Winter*, pp. 602–6. For a detailed description of the events and meetings leading up to MacArthur's dismissal, see chapter 28, pp. 477–90, in authorized biography by Forest C. Pogue, *Marshall*. For the meetings leading to the dismissal, see Truman, *Years of Hope*, pp. 446–48, and Acheson, *Present*, pp. 521–22 and 526–27. See Betts, *Soldiers*, pp. 19, 54, and Spanier, *Truman*, p. 4.

12   McCullough, *Truman*, p. 794.

Generals Marshall and MacArthur in Cairo,
one of the rare meetings of the two.

had withheld it until April 9. Although he wanted the maximum information to bolster his decision and in the end was supported unanimously by his inner staff, the president was determined that this be his decision as commander-in-chief, not the result of a consensus at the top. "This is my decision and my decision alone."[13]

---

13   Halberstam, *Coldest Winter*, p. 605. Brands, *General*, p. 303. To help him make up his mind, the president dispatched an aide to the Library

Marshall was sensitive to suggestions that he might seek MacArthur's dismissal out of some kind of long-standing vendetta toward the legendary commander. Marshall utterly rejected this, calling it "damn nonsense." The two generals had no "relationship," having met only three times. The last time was when MacArthur returned to Washington, DC, after being fired. MacArthur had considered Marshall the best colonel in the Army. He had recommended him for his first star in 1935 and for his sensitive assignment to Chicago to command the National Guard division. During the Second World War, Marshall had always supported MacArthur and had been his greatest backer in the nation's capital. The fact that Marshall had been appointed Chief of Staff in 1939 over the heads of several dozen higher-ranking generals owes a lot to MacArthur. Both generals wanted to get rid of the rigid seniority system and to promote officers on the basis of merit. Marshall could at times express criticism of MacArthur. In a meeting of the two soldiers years before the dismissal, MacArthur had referred to "my staff." Marshall interrupted him, saying "You don't have a staff, General. You have a court."[14]

The two meetings on April 6 to discuss the situation were attended by Marshall, Acheson, Harriman, and Bradley. The president was present at the first one. In the morning session following a cabinet meeting, Truman asked his advisers what should be done about MacArthur's "open defiance of the president." He remembered suggesting to Marshall that he review all correspondence with MacArthur. He also wrote later that he had already decided to recall him, but that he

of Congress to research Abraham Lincoln's firing of General George McClellan in 1862. *New York Times*, April 15, 2018.

14   Speech at the George C. Marshall Foundation by Jim Zobel, head of the MacArthur museum and archives in Norfolk, Virginia. September 14, 2017. Quote about "court" in Halberstam, *Coldest Winter*, p. 373.

desired additional consultation with his close advisers before finalizing his decision. The defense secretary advocated caution. He opposed MacArthur's immediate relief. He and General Bradley both feared that a firing of the general would adversely affect the military appropriation bill being considered by Congress.

The afternoon meeting on April 6 took place in Marshall's office and was attended by Acheson, Harriman, and Bradley. Marshall proposed bringing MacArthur home for consultation and a stern talk before reaching a final decision. He asked the other gentlemen what their opinions of this suggestion were. Secretary of State Acheson asserted that "we were all strongly opposed." He favored immediate dismissal and found this a horrible suggestion. In full uniform and with the full panoply of his four commands, the commander would apply all his theatrical skill to sway public opinion in the wrong way. Regardless of how the matter would be handled, Acheson warned the president: "You will have the biggest fight of your administration." Marshall did not want the military to be in the midst of such a fight. All agreed to recommend to the president when they would meet with him the following morning "that he not make his decision until we had all thought about it over the weekend."[15]

Marshall accepted the criticism and withdrew his recommendation. He agreed to Truman's request to review all messages that had gone back and forth between Washington and MacArthur to see whether there had been insubordination. He concluded that there had been. However, given the imprecise nature of the orders sent to MacArthur, insubordination and violation of a direct JCS order might be hard to prove. Disobedience of the president's December 5/6 directive to clear all public statements was indisputable. Above all, Marshall

---

15   Halberstam, *Coldest Winter*, pp. 604–6. Quote on page 604. Acheson, *Present*, pp. 521–22.

wanted more time for all the players to "cogitate" over what action should be taken.

At the Saturday morning April 7 meeting with his advisers, the president told Marshall to learn from the JCS what each of their opinions was "from a purely military point of view." Marshall privately agreed with Bradley that they should send "a personal and confidential letter to MacArthur" making clear how he was putting the government in a difficult position. The two leaders produced a draft, but they tore it up and never sent it.[16] On Sunday afternoon April 8, the chiefs met among themselves for an hour. When their discussion had ended, they went to Marshall's office for an hour. The secretary listened individually to the chiefs' opinions without expressing his own view.

On the morning of April 9, the group and Vice President Alban W. Barkley met again with the president. Truman had requested Marshall to ascertain the opinion of the JCS. Marshall did so that same evening. Bradley reported the group's unanimous conclusion that "from a purely military point of view" MacArthur should be relieved. Marshall was the last of Truman's inner circle to be persuaded that MacArthur had to go.[17] He finally revealed his own opinion on April 9 that he agreed with the JCS. However, he emphasized that the JCS conclusion was an opinion, not a recommendation. At this April 9 meeting, he went to each of the chiefs and asked him if he concurred with the decision; each did. After listening silently to the discussion, Truman finally revealed his own decision that the general must be dismissed. He later wrote that he had come to this conclusion two weeks earlier when MacArthur had preempted the UN call for truce talks. At a meeting in the afternoon of April 10, President Truman signed the orders to be

16 *Marshall Papers*, Vol. 7, pp. 478–80.

17 James/Wells, *Refighting*, pp. 216–17.

forwarded to MacArthur. The text was released to Ridgway the next day, April 11, informing him of his new command.

All had agreed with Bradley that MacArthur would be replaced by Lieutenant General Ridgway, with headquarters in Tokyo, and that Lieutenant General James A. Van Fleet, another "Marshall man" along with Ridgway and Eisenhower, would replace Ridgway as Eighth Army commander, the highest command in Korea itself. The process was made somewhat more complicated administratively by the fact that MacArthur had four separate commands: supreme commander for the Allied powers in Japan, commander-in-chief of UN forces, US commander-in-chief in the Far East, and commanding general of US Army forces in the Far East.[18]

It was Truman's intent that the fired general be treated with dignity. It was important that the commander in Tokyo be properly informed before the news became public. Secretary of the Army Frank Pace was in Korea, but he could not get to Tokyo in time to present a letter informing MacArthur of his dismissal. In the meantime, Truman mistakenly thought that the *Chicago Tribune* had received a leak and would publish the story before it could be officially announced. Therefore the president announced a press conference for 1:00 a.m., April 11, an unheard of time for such a press gathering. He announced that MacArthur "is unable to give his wholehearted support to the policies of the United States government and of the United Nations." "Military commanders must be governed by the policies and directives issued to them in a manner provided by our laws and Constitution." Truman never doubted that he had done the right thing. He later said less publicly that "I didn't fire him because he was a dumb son of a bitch, although he

---

18   *Marshall Papers*, Vol. 7, document 284. Brands, *General*, p. 288. Condit, *Test*, p. 105. The first thing that Ridgway reportedly did was to put a telephone in his office. MacArthur had refused to have one there.

was." "I fired him because he wouldn't respect the authority of the president."

The news was broadcast in Japan. MacArthur learned of it while at lunch with guests. An aide passed the shocking news to him via his wife. When Ridgeway arrived from Korea, MacArthur excoriated the president, questioning his mental stability and declaring that Truman was showing signs of bewilderment and confusion of thought. The general vowed to return to the US and "raise hell" against Truman's unwise and dangerous policies. He made good on that promise.[19]

Up to an estimated one million admiring and grateful Japanese lined the streets on that early morning of April 16 to bid farewell to their supreme benign authority and de facto emperor. First he had conquered them; then he resurrected them. Marshall played only a minor role in these reforms. However, he gained support for the creation of a new Japanese military establishment, known as the "police reserve" of 75,000 members.

---

19   Brands, *General*, pp. 303–6. Halberstam, *Coldest Winter*, p. 606. The April 23, 1951, edition of *Time* magazine, pp. 23–33, had a picture of Truman on the cover with the quote: "We do not want to widen the conflict." It cited the prestigious *Frankfurter Allgemeine Zeitung*: "The whole world stopped breathing for a moment over his fall." In the Communist world "jubilation was mostly high and unrestrained." There was "a vast sigh of relief" in Britain and Europe, "where MacArthur had long been the symbol of an American urge to get entangled in Asia, plunge into World War III." The British House of Commons cheered when the news was broken. There was less joy in Japan, where the *Nippon Times* wrote: "The Japanese owe General MacArthur an eternal debt of gratitude." *Newsweek*, on April 23, 1951, pp. 21–24, reported that "Washington was a bedlam." Truman quote in Sides, *On Desperate Ground*, p. 336. Senator Joe McCarthy declared the dismissal "the greatest victory the Communists have ever won." Hitchcock, *Eisenhower*, pp. 53–54. *Time* magazine reported that when General Eisenhower, who was reviewing French troops, got the news, he uttered, "Well, I'll be damned." As NATO commander, Eisenhower never publicly criticized Truman even though he disagreed with the president on some domestic and foreign policies.

This grew to 254,799 by 1960. Its officers had served in the imperial armed forces during the Second World War. Marshall supported the peace treaty with Japan and the mutual security agreement that followed.[20]

After a night in Hawaii, MacArthur's party proceeded to San Francisco, where the largest audience the general had ever seen assembled to welcome him home. The defense secretary was joined by the three service secretaries and the Joint Chiefs to greet MacArthur's plane upon arrival at National Airport (now Ronald Reagan Washington National Airport) in Washington. A half of a million admirers poured onto the mall to catch a glimpse of the hero, who was welcomed by a seventeen-gun salute. A military band played, and countless veterans' groups were present. The city had not seen anything like this since General Dwight D. Eisenhower had returned following V-E Day.

Republicans and Democrats alike wanted the general to speak to a joint session of Congress on April 19, so Marshall extended the invitation.[21] The House chamber was wired by all the national radio networks, and it was prepared for a more limited television broadcast. Few people ever forgot what they heard that day. There were war, politics and nostalgia in his speech. "Those who claim our strength is inadequate to protect on both fronts—the Asian as well as the European— "are "defeatists." "You cannot appease or otherwise surrender to communism in Asia without simultaneously undermining our efforts to halt its advance in Europe."

The entry of a new enemy, the Chinese, into the war demanded a "drastic revision of strategic planning," but that was not forthcoming. Such measures as an economic and naval blockade of China, the "removal of restrictions on air

---

20   For the many accomplishments MacArthur achieved in Japan, see Brands, *General*, pp. 13–20.

21   *Marshall Papers*, Vol. 7, document 287.

reconnaissance of China's coastal area and of Manchuria," and a lifting of restrictions on the use of Chinese National troops were necessary. He incorrectly stretched the truth by saying that these views had been fully shared by "practically every military concerned with the Korean campaign, including our own Joint Chiefs of Staff." That most certainly did not include Marshall.

The circumstances he described "forbade victory." Leading into his most famous line, he stated that "war's very object is victory, not prolonged indecision. In war there is no substitute for victory." "Appeasement but begets new and bloodier war." He did not say a single word about the main reason he was recalled: he had erased the line that separates politics from military advice.

In closing his fifty-two years of military service, he quoted from a popular old barrack ballad: "Old soldiers never die; they just fade away." Senators and congressmen from both sides of the aisle leapt to their feet and rewarded the old soldier with excited and prolonged applause.

Truman neither listened to nor watched the speech. He was aware that the enthusiastic response was a sign of just how unhappy many Americans were with him. This was made even more obvious a few days later when an estimated seven and a half million New Yorkers attended the largest ticker-tape parade in Manhattan's history to honor the returning hero. His open car slowly proceeded through fifteen miles of city streets while steamboats and tugs in New York harbor sounded off, and fireboats shot jet streams in the air. A host of marching bands blew their triumphant music. A year later, in April 1952, the House of Representatives debated impeaching Truman for sending troops to Korea under UN command without congressional approval, for dismissing MacArthur, and for seizing America's steel mills to prevent a worker strike during the Korean conflict.[22]

---

22 Brands, *General*, pp. 318–328. Hitchcock, *Eisenhower*, pp. 54–55. *New York Times*, December 1, 2019, p. 20.

CONGRESSIONAL HEARINGS

On April 25, 1951, the Senate voted unanimously to have its Armed Services and Foreign Relations Committees conduct joint closed hearings dealing with the relief of General MacArthur. Daily transcripts of uncensored testimony were made available to the press and public. However, classified information was exorcised from the published reports. MacArthur was scheduled to go first, from May 3–5, followed by Marshall from May 7–14.

Shortly before the hearings commenced, the administration leaked to the *New York Times* a summary of the stenographer's transcript of the talks on Wake Island, followed later by the full transcript. These contained the general's assurance to the president that the Chinese would not enter the war in Korea and that if they did, they would face "the greatest slaughter." Truman was told with confidence that the war would be over soon and that troops could be sent from Korea to Europe. Although he denied that there had been an official stenographic report, MacArthur's reputation as a military genius became somewhat tarnished by his unfounded predictions, which by then everybody knew to be misguided and misleading.[23]

The general ended his testimony with dramatic and impassioned statements about his notion of warfare that was so different from that of the president and his defense secretary, who accepted the reality of limited war in the Cold War era: "War, never before in the history of the world, has been applied in a piece-meal way, that you make half-war, and not whole war. Now that China is using the maximum of her force against us is quite evident. And we are not using the maximum of ours against her. The inertia that exists! There is no policy—there is

---

23 Hitchcock, *Eisenhower*, pp. 329–30, 341–42. *Time* called MacArthur "a man of enormous certainty in a time of uncertainties." "The MacArthur Hearing," May 14, 1951, pp. 19–25.

nothing, I tell you, no plan or anything." "That is not war. That is appeasement."[24]

Marshall was not looking forward to his testifying May 7–14. He admitted in a May 3 letter that "all of this business is most unpalatable" and that there are "ulterior purposes behind almost every action and question. However, I am somewhat accustomed to this but I can't claim to enjoy it." He met with Acheson, Harriman, and the JCS to get ready for his testimony, which lasted almost twenty-eight hours and filled over 400 pages.

Marshall opened in a gracious way, confessing that "it is a very distressing necessity, a very distressing occasion that compels me to appear here this morning and in effect in almost direct opposition to a great many of the views and actions of General MacArthur. He is a brother Army officer, a man for whom I have tremendous respect as to his military capabilities and military performances and from all I can learn, as to his administration of Japan." The two generals had never been friends, and some persons considered them to be competitors. This put Marshall into a delicate position because the dismissal of MacArthur might be interpreted as one five-star general eliminating another, his long-standing rival. The fact was that Marshall always gave MacArthur full support.[25]

According to *Time*, the "wise and tired old George Marshall" disputed MacArthur doggedly, point-by-point in his hearing. Marshall corrected a mistake by MacArthur: there had never been a disagreement between himself, Truman, and the JCS. By contrast there were fundamental differences of judgment between MacArthur and the president, secretary of defense, and the JCS.

---

24   Brands, *General*, pp. 344–345.

25   *Marshall Papers*, Vol. 7, pp. 500–501. Condit, *Test*, pp. 77, 88–89, 104, 107–8. Both Marshall and the JCS opposed the court martial of MacArthur. James/Wells, *Refighting*, p. 213. For their opinion of the "Big General," see p. 23.

Also, MacArthur was completely wrong in asserting that the defense secretary had overruled the JCS in their opposition to handing Formosa over to the PRC and giving the Chinese Communists a seat in the UN. The general had cited a January 12, 1951, memorandum to show that the JCS had been in agreement with him on the subject of stronger measures against China. Marshall made it clear that that document contained tentative courses of action to be applied only in a future emergency; that necessity never came about.[26]

In reference to MacArthur's disagreement with the president, the JCS and himself on the objectives sought in Korea, Marshall reiterated that the administration's goal was to defeat aggression and restore peace. "We have persistently sought to confine the conflict to Korea and to prevent its spreading into a third world war." Most UN allies supported this, and "our efforts have succeeded in thwarting the aggressions in Korea, and in stemming the tide of aggression in Southeast Asia and elsewhere throughout the world. Our efforts in Korea have given us some sorely needed time and impetus to accelerate the building of our defenses and those of our allies against the threatened onslaught of Soviet imperialism." He criticized MacArthur for wanting to risk spreading the fight to the Chinese homeland and to an all-out war with the Soviet Union even if this led to America's loss of allies and exposed Western Europe to attack. While

---

26   *Time*, May 14, 1951, pp. 19, 24–25. On May 18, 1951, *U.S. News & World Report*, pp. 19–21, published an article, "ABCs of the Big Debate." It detailed the Marshall–MacArthur debate point-by-point. In addition to undermining the president's truce efforts on March 24, 1951, MacArthur "carried out military orders but publically objected to policies agreed on with our allies, such as the ban against following planes across the border. This endangered our relations with allied nations. And it hurts morale for the commander in the field to emphasize the number of troops that are dying." In its April 20, 1951, issue, *U.S. News & World Report* published, on p. 21, "Truman vs MacArthur: Blow by Blow," itemizing their disagreements.

MacArthur dismissed the likelihood of Soviet intervention without providing evidence for his opinion. Marshall considered it "a very real possibility." A few politburo members could decide quickly to go to war whenever they choose.

What brought about the need to remove MacArthur from his four commands was his public disagreement with US foreign and military policy. His differences of opinion became so strong that there was "grave doubt" whether he should be allowed to make decisions that a theater commander would normally make. In this situation there was no other recourse but to relieve him. Asked to cite a specific example of how MacArthur had undermined US policy, Marshall mentioned his March 24 scuttling of the president's imminent call for peace talks.

Marshall also cited the general's letter to Speaker Joseph Martin. Asked if a senator or congressman is entitled to a frank reply from a military man of decision-making authority, Marshall answered curtly, "No, sir." A commander must "exercise considerable discretion" and cannot involve himself in a public "criticism of the commander-in-chief to any congressman of either party."[27] In later congressional testimony on July 2, 1951, Marshall reiterated his belief "that we would not become involved in fighting on the mainland of Asia." He added that "we should not lessen our efforts for the defense of Europe because of the Pacific."[28]

As Marshall's testimony ended, many Americans believed he had delivered a knock-out blow. *The Oregonian* in Portland wrote on May 8, 1951, that "General Marshall is trusted by Congress to a degree unrivaled by anyone else in government because of his masterful grasp of military and foreign problems,

---

27   *Marshall Papers*, Vol. 7, pp. 499–516. Brands, *General*, pp. 353–58. Condit, *Test*, p. 103.

28   *Marshall Papers*, Vol. 7, pp. 576–77. Condit, *Test*, pp. 103–8. James/ Wells, *Refighting*, p. 208.

his forthright honesty and sincerity, and his lack of interest in political goals." In a May 21, 1951, editorial, *The Detroit News* wrote that his performance was "an impressive example of patient forbearance and grasp of the situation....When he was finished, no room remained for public doubt as to where he stood....He and the Joint Chiefs had all along been opposed to the strategic arguments advanced by General MacArthur for widening the war in Asia...because they believed them to be militarily unsound."

Marshall had frequently been the target of outrageous verbal abuse. The worst attacks were launched by Indiana Senator William E. Jenner and his Republican colleague from Wisconsin, Senator Joseph R. McCarthy. During the debate over Marshall's confirmation in September 1950, Jenner had called him "a front man for traitors" and "a living lie."

Secretary of State Dean Acheson came next. As the administration's most polarizing figure and a particular target of Truman critics for "losing China" and failing to include Korea in his January 1950 National Press Club speech, he experienced a particular diminution of civility during his thirty-eight hours of testifying.

General Omar Bradley denied that the JCS agreed with MacArthur's desire to take the war to the Chinese homeland: "The Joint Chiefs of Staff believe that these same measures do increase the risk of global war and that such a risk should not be taken unnecessarily." He continued: "Under present circumstances, we have recommended against enlarging the war." He ended with the most quotable and compelling sentence uttered during the entire hearing process: "Frankly, in the opinion of the Joint Chiefs of Staff, [MacArthur's] strategy would involve us in the wrong war, in the wrong place, at the wrong time and with the wrong enemy."[29]

---

29   Brands, *General*, pp. 358–62.

On June 14, 1951, McCarthy rose on the senate floor for more than three hours to deliver a scathing attack on the defense secretary. Only a handful of senators showed up to sit through his tirade. He claimed that Marshall had made common cause with Stalin since 1943 and was, along with Acheson, the leader of "a conspiracy so immense and an infamy so black as to dwarf any previous such venture in the history of man." In its August 18, 1951, issue, *Colliers* wrote that this speech "sets a new high for irresponsibility in a senatorial career distinguished mainly for its extravagant accusations." The magazine found it "incredible that any American who is both sane and honest can believe that George Marshall or Dean Acheson is a traitorous hireling of the Kremlin. We do not think the Washington Republicans believe it. So why have they not repudiated Mr. McCarthy's charges?"

McCarthy published this vituperative attack on Marshall in a book titled *America's Retreat from Victory: The Story of George Catlett Marshall*. Marshall was careful not to respond or comment on such personal political attacks. In an interview with John Sutherland published posthumously in the November 2, 1959, issue of *US News & World Report*, Marshall stated that "those who come out with irresponsible charges against me are trying to create issues so they can keep their jobs. It's politics. They are afraid of being defeated in polls and they look for issues. I believe we could have a more responsible Congress if these politicians weren't so worried about keeping their jobs."

Marshall's authorized biographer, Forrest Pogue, suggested that such charges may have strengthened his decision to retire as soon as was feasible. While a candidate for the presidency in 1952, Eisenhower was pressed by the media to respond to these outrageous allegations. But because McCarthy enjoyed considerable popularity within certain elements of the Republican party, Ike hesitated to utter criticism of the Wisconsin senator in public. In a late August 1952 press conference, he finally spoke out: "General Marshall is one of the patriots and anyone who has lived with him, worked with him as I have, knows that he is a man of real selflessness.... [There is] nothing of disloyalty in General Marshall's soul."

A few weeks later, Eisenhower stumbled badly by deleting from a speech delivered in McCarthy's presence in his home state of Wisconsin a paragraph boldly praising Marshall. He felt that the electoral stakes were so high that he needed to shore up his support from the party's right wing and Old Guard. Since the original text of the speech had already been distributed to the press with the paragraph of praise in it, he was accused of having caved in to a demagogue and was severely criticized for it. Marshall, who had already retired a year earlier, offered no comment. But Eisenhower regretted his decision the rest of his life.[30]

MARSHALL'S LAST MONTHS IN OFFICE

By mid-May 1951, the overall military situation in Korea was favorable for the UN allies. Marshall noted in his remarks at the National Armed Forces Day Banquet on May 18 that the North Korean army had been destroyed. The Chinese Communist military had been dealt "terrific blows," and its prestige was seriously damaged. "The defense system of the entire Pacific has been invigorated." Marshall presided over a three-fold increase in defense spending. This gave the US military options other than nuclear war. The strength of the US armed forces had by March 21, 1951, been doubled to over 2.9 million men and women since the war began; an additional 500,000 troops were in uniform three months later. This was a faster mobilization than Marshall had guided from 1940–1942. Truman called this

---

30 *Marshall Papers*, Vol. 7, pp. 555–56. Pogue, *Marshall*, pp. 489–90. Stoler, *Marshall*, p. 190. Acheson, *Present*, p. 365. Condit, *Test*, pp. 107–8. Thomas C. Reeves, *The Life and Times of Joe McCarthy*, pp. 278, 322. Hitchcock, *Eisenhower*, pp. 75–76, 80–82. *Words of George C. Marshall*, p. 100.

an "all-time record rate." He also stated that "I am confident that under your wise leadership the Department of Defense will continue to build the strength we need, fully supported by the Congress, and by the American people." The decision to fight in Korea had given life to the UN and helped get NATO up and running; both were successes.[31]

The manpower and industrial mobilization that enabled the nation to send troops to Europe and to fight in Korea had been started by Marshall's predecessor as secretary of defense, Louis Johnson. It was made especially challenging because all plans had hitherto operated under the assumption that future wars would be all-out, not limited. Selective Service had been extended for one year on July 9, 1950. The Defense Production Act came into being on September 8, 1950, two weeks before Marshall was sworn in.

Writing in the *Washington Post* on November 17, 1950, Stewart Alsop described what he saw as the different approaches Johnson and Marshall took toward funding a stronger US military. Johnson assumed that any defense expenditure would ruin the American economy. By contrast, Marshall and Lovett figured out what the country needs, and then they took a hard look at the costs in men and money. What they decided on was a twenty-division army with 1.5 million soldiers, an air force quickly expanded to ninety groups, a navy in war readiness with a much more powerful air arm, and a Marine force. In November 1950, Marshall submitted to the president a "stupendous" $45 billion rearmament budget as part of the overall $72 billion budget for fiscal year beginning July 1, 1951. This was nearly double the figure for the preceding year. The titles of newspaper articles reveal what Marshall's constant message was: "Marshall

31 *Marshall Papers*, Vol. 7, document 269 and pp. 525–26. Marshall Library, Xerox 3293. Cray, *General*, p. 725. *New York Times*, March 22, 1951.

Urges Enduring Defense, Decries Public's Vacillation in Past" and "Marshall Hits 'Feast and Famine' Policy of US Defense Plans."[32]

Marshall was on the job on December 8, 1950, when the president declared a national emergency. Truman created an Office of Defense Mobilization as a coordinating agency. The Department of Defense was responsible for planning, directing, and implementing the military production program. Marshall was determined to keep the industrial mobilization limited so that it would not cripple the nation's economy after the end of hostilities. "Don't plunge into this until it is absolutely necessary." All this was well within his capability. He liked to say that thanks to his experience during the Second World War, he "had a PhD in mobilization."[33]

TRIP TO KOREA

The Evening Star reported on June 8, 1951, that Marshall said he had made a short trip to Korea and Tokyo to "congratulate our Army leaders." More importantly, he decided to see for himself how the war was going. He no doubt wanted to get an accurate impression whether the time was right to enter peace negotiations. But in his closing press conference he insisted that his purpose for making the whirlwind trip to Korea was strictly military. He refused to use the term "stalemate" to describe the situation in Korea. "Whenever we start something and don't finish it the same afternoon, in our country that's a stalemate." Only three weeks later, on July 2, the Chinese commander

---

32 *New York Post*, November 27, 1950. *New York Times*, November 25, 1950. *Washington Post*, November 25, 1950.

33 Robert W. Coakley, *Highlights of Mobilization Korean War*, pp. 2–6. Marshall Library, Xerox 3291. First quote in "Defense Chief's Basic Plan," *U.S. News & World Report*, December 29, 1950. Second quote in Marshall Library, Box 218 Scrapbook.

responded favorably to General Ridgway's message expressing readiness for negotiations.[34]

Before he could embark on his journey to Korea, the defense secretary endured a grueling Senate hearing on MacArthur's firing, and he delivered commencement addresses to West Point, where he talked about the citizen's army that must support democracy, the Naval Academy, and Washington University in St. Louis. At the latter institution on June 6, 1951, he praised General Ridgway: "What has happened since General Ridgway assumed command of the Eighth Army has not only struck a deadly blow to the prestige of the Communists in Asia, but has all but wrecked their pride and morale in the debacle of the past month in Korea." "We have posed a terrific problem for the hostile regime in China." He reiterated his support for Universal Military Training (UMT) to prevent in the future the "much too rapid—almost tumultuous demobilization" of America's armed forces at the end of the Second World War. This sank the US "into a position of military impotence at a time when...we were accorded the responsibility of leadership in the world." He expressed relief that the "unusually difficult and dangerous situations" the US has faced have been managed without general war.[35]

Marshall wanted his departure to be secret so that the press would not be involved. Therefore, as soon as he had delivered

---

34 Acheson, *Present*, pp. 534–35. Appleman, *Ridgway*, p. 559. Marshall quote in "How Long is an Afternoon," *New York Daily News*, June 9, 1951. In the midst of his 1952 presidential campaign, Eisenhower pledged on October 24 to "go to Korea" and to do everything in his power either to win or end the conflict on that peninsula. The voters cheered, and many journalists were convinced: "That does it—Ike is in." It was unclear exactly what he planned to do in Korea. However, after winning a dramatically lopsided victory on November 4—55 percent of the popular vote and 442 electoral college votes—Eisenhower went. A half of a year later, an armistice was achieved. Hitchcock, *Eisenhower*, pp. 82–83.

35 *Marshall Papers*, Vol. 7, document 313 and pp. 548–51.

*Marshall in Korea, June 8, 1951. Standing behind
Marshall is LTG William M. Hoge.*

his commencement address to the 1,900 new graduates of
Washington University in St. Louis, he swapped planes so that
people would think he was returning to Washington. He flew
to Korea via Tacoma, the Aleutian Islands in Alaska and Tokyo,
arriving in Seoul on June 8, 1951. Thus began a "fast and furious
trip to Korea, which was interesting, informative, and tiring." In
1914, while on leave from his duty station in the Philippines, he

had visited Korea and Japan to inspect battlefields of the 1904–1905 Russo-Japanese War. His 1951 voyage was his last visit to an active battlefront.

After flying to I Corps in horrible weather conditions for his first headquarter visit, General Ridgway, whom Marshall admired and probably considered the best general in the American armed forces, suggested they continue by jeep. Marshall liked the small plane at their disposal and would not hear of remaining on the ground. The pilots shuttered at the prospect of flying through such a storm. But as Ridgway's public relations officer, James Quirk, remembered, they "agreed that if the Old Man could do it so could they. It was so dangerous it was silly but Generals are like that." By the end of the visit, Marshall had spoken with Eighth Army Commander General Hoyt Van Fleet and all corps commanders, most division commanders and all but two of the commanders of foreign units deployed on the peninsula. The defense secretary enjoyed the hazardous flying in the small aircraft so much that he used one to commute between Leesburg and the Pentagon for the rest of his time in office.

Ridgway and Marshall discussed military policy and operations, manpower, Ridgway's assignment, and the potential for peace talks. At a concluding press conference in Tokyo, Marshall denied that the war was a stalemate. Morale was high, and the Eighth Army was probably "the most ably trained Army we ever had." Chinese troops had been battered, but they still sought to expel American forces from Korea in order "to be in a better position to attack Japan." America was planning "for a long period" to deal with this threat. Marshall departed at 3:00 p.m. on June 11 and was back in Washington the next day. During his seven-day trip, he had spent only a little over six hours in Korea.[36]

---

36   Ridgway, *Korean War*, p. 193. Condit, *Test*, p. 114. *Marshall Papers*, Vol. 7, pp. 547–51. See documents 338 and 339, July 16 and 18, for

He expressed his thoughts on the way to dissuade the Soviet Union from seeking its goals by military means. He proposed that "we appear before the world as determined, implacably determined, to get ourselves in such a strong position that the Kremlin will not dare to upset the peace of the world." He argued that this would be a more effective deterrent than any weapons system, including atomic weapons. The threat of an all-out war continued; it was even increasing, as seen in the enemy's build-up. In Korea, the war remained limited and resulted in a stalemate.[37]

FINALE OF A SOLDIER'S CAREER

The finale of Marshall's half century of service to his country was coming ever nearer. He was seventy years of age and not in the best of health. When he quipped that one could not get any productivity out of a man after 3:00 p.m., he was no doubt thinking of his own diminishing stamina and energy. He shortened the working hours in the Pentagon. He found the Pentagon personnel "overworked decidedly to such a degree that it has awakened my concern." He found it inefficient "to hold them to their desks over longer hours without adequate tasks." He continued: "When there is work to do, they do it. And when there is not work to do, I would not be one to insist that they hang around."[38]

When Marshall went to work, he never experienced a day when there was "no work to do." In addition to his official duties as secretary, he assumed numerous responsibilities that were not written into his job description. From July 1, 1946, he served

---

his praise of General Van Fleet, who had done a "masterful job" in executing his counter-offensive.

37   Pogue, *Marshall*, pp. 487–88. Sides, *On Desperate Ground*, p. 336.

38   *Marshall Papers*, Vol. 7, document 196. Pogue, *Marshall*, p. 413.

on the VMI Board of Visitors at his alma mater in Lexington, Virginia. He was elected the Board's president on September 23, 1950, a mere two days after being sworn in as defense secretary. He attended all scheduled meetings until his resignation as president on January 15, 1951.

Known to his "Brother Rat" classmates by his VMI nickname "Pug," he enjoyed receiving from them and other friends a flood of newspaper clippings from the local *Rockbridge County News* telling of his fifty-yard touchdown run as a six-foot tall, 150-pound tackle on the cadet football team. He intimated that "the ball I am carrying today is a little heavier than the ordinary football, but the goal is the same." He also admitted that "it is hard to believe now that I ever ran fifty yards with eleven intent young men trying to stop me!" He was named to the All-Southern team. He was First Captain of the corps, but he was not a brilliant student, finishing fifteenth in a class of thirty-four. As was the practice at military academies at the time, he did not receive a bachelor's degree.

He was honored at a Marshall Day Celebration at VMI on May 15, 1951. The event was attended by the 750-man Corps of Cadets and a crowd of 8,000 admirers. This was the commemoration of the Civil War cadets' participation in the 1864 Battle of New Market. As he reviewed the cadet parade, he put his hand with hat over his heart rather than saluting. Marshall remembered it as "a perfect day in every respect."[39]

An arch into the barracks was dedicated to the general, and Barnard Baruch was the featured speaker. In his own address to the Corps of Cadets, Marshall noted that when he was a cadet in Lexington, there was no movie theater, no automobiles, and nothing to do. To provide the cadets with some understanding of the changed world they were entering, he spoke about how far back in time his cadetship and soldier's career went. He entered

---

39   *Marshall Papers*, Vol. 7, documents 182, 190, 300, pp. 173, 518–19.

VMI in September 1897. Only eight months later, the Battle of Manila Bay took place. Admiral Dewey sank the Spanish fleet, and "for the first time the United States stepped into the international picture." The independence campaign in Cuba and the Philippine insurrection flared.[40]

He played a part in the work of the American Battle Monuments Commission, of which he was chairman. It dealt mainly with military cemeteries.[41] He supported and testified for the implementation of the St. Lawrence Seaway and power project with Canada.[42] He advocated for an increase of women in various aspects of a national emergency. Their numbers had doubled during the Korean War.[43] He called on Latin American nations to step up their self-help and mutual aid in order to be capable of fending off and defeating aggression and deploying troops to Korea.[44]

Marshall accepted scores of invitations to give speeches and be interviewed. In June 1951, he gave graduation addresses at West Point, the Naval Academy, and Washington University in St. Louis. He turned down twenty-eight additional invitations.[45] He crowned the Queen of the Apple Blossom Festival, the daughter of UN Secretary General Trygve Lie, in Winchester, Virginia, on May 4, 1951. He also invited paper boys from all over America to visit him in his office.

Although Truman had ordered in 1948 equality for African Americans in the armed forces, 90 percent of black soldiers in

---

40   *Marshall Papers*, Vol. 7, document 300.

41   *Marshall Papers*, Vol. 7, documents 177, 264, 356.

42   *Marshall Papers*, Vol. 7, document 245.

43   *Marshall Papers*, Vol. 7, document 247.

44   *Marshall Papers*, Vol. 7, document 252.

45   *Marshall Papers*, Vol. 7, documents 313, 314.

Korea fought in racially segregated units. However, the desperate need for manpower obligated the army to assign black soldiers to previously all-white units. General Ridgway considered racial segregation of military units to be "un-American and un-Christian." He officially requested permission to integrate his command. Marshall oversaw studies of how racially mixed units fared in battle. Segregation formally ended in the Far East Command by July 1951, but it continued to exist in other army units. New York Congressman, then Senator Jacob K. Javits was a real driver in ridding the military of racial segregation.[46]

From July 28 to August 24, 1951, Marshall took a much needed leave in Waquoit, Massachusetts. When President Truman had first asked him in September 1950 to be the third secretary of defense, he had agreed to serve for six months. The president later requested that the general serve until the last day of June, 1951, and later until September 1. There was always an emergency or legislation pending in Congress critical to the defense department that made it inopportune for him to leave. In the end Marshall stayed until September 12, 1951. The public was not informed about these deliberations and could only speculate about how long Marshall would remain in office. His trusted deputy, Robert A. Lovett, replaced him a few weeks later. Marshall praised Lovett as "a superb helmsman. I know he will keep the ship headed into the wind and on an even keel."[47]

46   *Marshall Papers*, Vol. 7, documents 275, 281, 340. James/Wells, *Refighting*, pp. 26–28. Sandler, *Korean War*, p. 252. Blair, *Forgotten War*. Doris Kearns Goodwin, *No Ordinary Time: Franklin and Elinor Roosevelt: The Home Front in World War II*, pp. 626–27. General Ned Almond believed to his dying day that African-Americans were poor soldiers and should be excluded from combat units. Sides, *On Desperate Ground*, pp. 42–44.

47   *Marshall Papers*, Vol. 7, document 364 and pp. 603, 629–33.

UNIVERSAL MILITARY TRAINING

An important reason why he remained in office longer than originally planned was that he wanted to do all he could to guide his pet project through the maze of Congress and the executive branch: Universal Military Training (UMT). He was deeply concerned about the American tradition of raising an army precipitously in time of crisis and then demobilizing after the war is over in a way that Marshall called "emasculation." This makes the US "impotent before the world." Surely America could come up with a mandatory system of training eighteen-year-old male citizen soldiers for four to six months. They would then serve in the National Guard or reserve while living and working in the civilian society. They would be prepared to defend their country when necessity called; none would be sent to war before his nineteenth birthday. He believed that such a policy of military preparedness and trained reserve strength was consistent with Americans' political values. In a speech to the American Association of School Administrators on February 19, 1951, he asserted that his proposal "is American in character and consistent with our principles of education. I think it is fair. I am certain that it is democratic. It would be universal in application. There would be no privileged groups because of birth or wealth."

Marshall was firmly convinced that UMT was a policy of peace. In his speech to the Women's Patriotic Conference on National Defense, January 25, 1951, he argued that "all agree that we must make every endeavor to maintain the peace. The question is, the problem is, how do we proceed in order to avoid wars? Clearly it must be evident to all these days that we must first develop, and then maintain strength, material as well as moral." What would make war improbable would be an American military posture that "commanded the respect of nations who threaten us today." The US will be so powerful that "its views on peace will be compelling." "From my own experience I can state that men of 18 are among our best soldiers. They are brave; they are strong." A man's eighteenth year requires the least dislocation in his life. He is probably not married, has no children, and has not yet begun his university studies. Such a large number of males who had been trained in the military arts would be an effective deterrent and make war less likely to occur. Marshall equated peace with military preparedness. He cited the example of George Washington and his colonial soldiers, who saw "some form of universal military training as a definite obligation of citizenship in our democracy." He also argued that UMT was the only way "we could financially manage a real effective posture of strength." The taxpayer would not be overburdened by it. He told the National Guard Association in a speech on October 24, 1950, that "we never can have a large standing Army....It isn't in keeping with our tradition and it isn't in keeping with our budget."[48]

He had advocated such UMT for over three decades as an "enduring system of national defense" that would discourage aggression. In 1943, in the midst of the Second World War, a bill was submitted to Congress to create it after the war was successfully won. But Americans reverted to habit. They demobilized four million men by the time of his retirement from the army in November 1945, and they made only limited plans for their new role as leader of the free world. Such leadership required "steel" in the form of military power. In a statement read to the American Legion on October 10, 1950, he had argued that "in the world today, I am sorry to say, military strength seems the most essential factor in the support of our foreign policy and of difficult negotiations, and it seems for the moment to be the best

48   *Marshall Papers*, Vol. 7, documents 151, 163, 214, 215, 285. For Washington quotes on citizen soldiers, who "are at all times ready for war," see p. 396. Speech by Mark Stoler at Marshall Foundation in Lexington, VA, October 18, 2017. Also *Words of George C. Marshall*, pp. 139, 140, 142. Quotes on peace, *Words*, pp.138, 182–83, and page 139 for George Washington.

means to prevent war." However, many citizens were convinced that atomic weapons had made large armies obsolete. Many also asked why UMT was needed when American soldiers were fighting so well in Korea by the spring of 1951.[49]

While Marshall was secretary of defense, UMT was again discussed in Congress as an attachment to the Selective Service Act. Truman gave his backing. Referring to Marshall's wish, Air Force Brigadier General A. Robert Ginsburgh, military assistant to the director of the office of public information in the defense department, stated that "it looks as though UMT is the big thing." Marshall put everything he had into making UMT a reality. He confided: "This is what I hope to see before I die."

It was on Marshall's watch that the Universal Military Training and Service Act of June 1951 had been extended until 1955. This lowered the draft age from nineteen to eighteen and a half, lengthened the term of service to twenty-four months, and required six additional years in the reserves. He greeted this as a step toward his cherished but ill-fated UMT. However, while Congress accepted the Selective Service Act, UMT again died in Congress. It was Marshall's worst disappointment during his year as secretary of defense.[50] It was never subsequently enacted despite his efforts.

FAREWELL

President Truman said his farewell words: "In again accepting your resignation from a position of high responsibility I realize how many times previously you have sought to retire to private

49 Stoler, *Marshall*, pp 143–44, 183–84. *Marshall Papers,* Vol. 7, pp. 462–63. Goodwin, *No Ordinary Time,* pp. 23–24. General Dwight D. Eisenhower also advocated UMT. See Hitchcock, *Eisenhower,* pp. 32–33.

50 *Marshall Papers,* Vol. 7, documents 114, 231. William Taylor, *Every Citizen a Soldier: The Campaign for Universal Military Training after World War II.*

life. But one time after another you have responded to a call to public service....To all of these offices you have brought great talent and wisdom. In fact, no man ever has given his country more distinguished and patriotic service than have you....You have earned your retirement many fold." Most of the news media were complimentary. Edward R. Morrow called him "the most self-controlled man I have ever known." Joseph C. Harsch said on radio that "obviously every Democrat in Washington commented in words of praise; more remarkably, most Republicans did the same."[51]

The war in Korea continued inconclusively for almost two years. The boundary between the two Koreas was basically where it had been when the war broke out. A demilitarized zone was created close to the 38th parallel. Formal negotiations began at Kaesong on July 10, 1951, and a cease fire went into effect on July 27. The venue was later moved to Panmunjom. Hundreds of meetings took place during the next two years. Fighting did not cease as both sides sought military advantages that would strengthen their hand in the negotiations. However, Eighth Army commander, General James A. Van Fleet, vehemently criticized the administration's prohibition of large-scale offensive operations after truce talks began.

The negotiations could have moved along faster and perhaps could have been settled before the 1952 elections if President Truman had not been so insistent that soldiers from the Communist north should have the freedom to be patriated in the south if they desired. Of 132,000 Chinese and North Korean prisoners in UN hands, only 70,000 wanted to be repatriated to the Communist north.[52]

The human consequences of the conflict cannot be ignored. According to Pentagon figures, more than 320,000 Americans

51   *Marshall Papers*, Vol. 7, pp. 629–30.

52   James/Wells, *Refighting*, pp. 21, 23, 73–75, 224–25.

served in the war; 33,651 Americans and 3,000 allied soldiers died, and more than 180,000 Chinese were killed. An estimated 2.5 million Korean civilians perished. This included roughly one-fourth of North Korea's population. Seoul changed hands four times. Half of South Koreans ended up living within fifty miles of the North. One-third of American prisoners of war died in the first year of the war. The armistice agreement of 1953 was not a peace treaty, and technically the war never ended. The two Koreas remained on a war footing ever since.

In his final weeks of office, Marshall was greatly involved in the discussions over the terms of negotiation and armistice. The issue was hotly discussed in the 1952 presidential elections. The Republican candidate, Dwight D. Eisenhower, who had been replaced as NATO's top commander by General Matthew Ridgway, announced that, if elected, he would go to Korea and devote himself to establishing peace there. He went, and the fighting stopped half a year later.

Eisenhower, who had served as MacArthur's chief of staff in the Philippines, had a high regard for MacArthur's intellect and theatrical skill. However, they had a serious falling out before the Second World War. Ike considered Marshall to be a man not easy to impress. He was cold and aloof, "remote and austere," a "man who forced everyone to keep his distance." Eisenhower always addressed Marshall as "general."[53]

The death of Stalin in March 1953 had left the Soviet Union with a new set of leaders who saw advantages in making peace in Korea. Generals from North Korea, China, and the United States signed the armistice in the summer of 1953 at Panmunjom, a village in what became the Demilitarized Zone (DMZ). It is 160 miles long and about 2.5 miles wide. It is a mere 35 miles from the South Korean capital, Seoul. It remains

---

53   Ambrose, *Soldier and President*, pp. 45, 62–67, 201–2, 269, 276, 282–84.

the world's most heavily armed border area. The South pledged to observe the cease-fire, but it did not sign because it had hopes of unifying the entire peninsula. Both the North and the South claim to be the rightful government of the entire Korean peninsula.

Although the two sides agreed to an armistice, no peace treaty, which would be a much more complicated political settlement, was ever achieved. In the twenty-first century, the US and other UN allies were technically still at war with a highly unstable, unpredictable and dangerous North Korea that is armed with nuclear weapons and the capability to deliver them to America's Asian allies and to the US mainland itself. Seven decades later, the United States still maintained 28,500 soldiers in Korea and continued to demand an accounting of the 7,700 missing service members, about 5,300 of whom are believed to be within North Korea.[54]

MARSHALL'S LEGACY

General George C. Marshall left an enduring legacy to his country and to the department of defense. His accomplishments as secretary of defense and lessons for his countrymen were many. He brought order into the running of the infant department of defense. He established an amical productive working relationship between the state and defense departments. By deferring to Secretary of State Dean Acheson in many ways, large and small, he strengthened the principle of civilian predominance over the military. He was a respected arbiter between the distinct services and thereby helped to reduce the traditional inter-service rivalries.

Marshall became the president's military affairs deputy. At no time was this more important than when General Douglas

---

54 *Marshall Papers*, Vol. 7, pp. 592–96. Brands, *General*, pp. 390, 394–95. James/Wells, *Refighting*, pp. 224–25.

MacArthur had to be relieved of his commands on April 11, 1951, for repeatedly and publicly criticizing the president's policies. Marshall did not initiate the recall of the popular general. But he organized the meetings that led up to the president's decision, and he supported it when it was adopted. Because of the trust Truman had for Marshall, and the fact that the defense secretary had a seat on the National Security Council, Marshall had considerable influence on international affairs at a very complicated and dangerous time for the United States. In that arena he skillfully balanced diplomatic and military concerns.

In office during wartime, he drew on his half of a century of military experience to enlighten the American public on war's realities. He was aware that America's military power was limited. That made it essential to use its power wisely and cautiously. He respected the military quality of the Chinese and Soviet soldiers. He knew better than to belittle or underestimate them and to take unnecessary risks by challenging an enemy whom one does not understand.

In Korea, Americans were involved in a very different kind of warfare than they had known only a half of a decade earlier. War in the Cold War era was necessarily limited. There could be no total war, no supreme victory, no complete and unconditional surrender. Atomic weapons, which the Soviet Union had developed by 1949, made total war almost unthinkable. Even impoverished North Korea ultimately developed nuclear weapons capable of reaching targets in the United States. War had become a matter of attrition, not annihilation.

He was defense secretary during America's first Cold War conflict. He succeeded in restoring the fighting power and confidence of the country's undersized and unprepared post-WWII armed forces. By April 1951, he had doubled their numbers. He also succeeded in preventing the national economy from being put on a total-war footing, which would have left the nation enlarged deficits and piles of unneeded left-over equipment. He made every effort to keep the war from expanding beyond the Korean peninsula. He repeatedly made it clear that the administration's policy was and should be "Europe first," as it had been in the Second World War and continued during and after the Cold War. This required an effective North Atlantic Treaty Organization (NATO), which he helped bring into being.

George C. Marshall served his country and the free world well as secretary of defense. Dean Acheson admired Marshall as one of few who accomplished something worthwhile and lasting against inertia. He wrote as Marshall departed that his presence "in the last year of grave peril to our country...steadied all of our vital actions and decisions."[55]

Marshall jotted down a few notes to tell the press on his final day, September 12, 1951. He mentioned the Japanese Peace Treaty, the completion of the report of the Commission on Universal Military Training, the Reserve Forces Bill's submission to Congress, and the readiness of his trusted subordinate, Robert Lovett, to continue his work as defense secretary. More than fifty years of uninterrupted service to the government "is just about as much as should be expected of one man—don't misunderstand me, I'm not complaining—I'm merely stating the fact of the matter." He concluded: "Now appears to be as appropriate a time as any to wind up 50 years of uninterrupted daily service to the government. I leave with very real regret, and with high devotion to the President and to the government."[56]

---

55   David S. McLellan, *Dean Acheson: The State Department Years*, pp. 33, 293, 315, 398. Quote in *Marshall Papers*, Vol. 7, p. 632.

56   *Marshall Papers*, Vol. 7, pp. 631–33. In Marshall's final days in office, a Security Treaty between the US and Philippines was signed on August 30, and the Japanese Peace Treaty was signed a week later. Marshall had little input into the latter.

Bibliography

BOOKS FOCUSING ON GEORGE C. MARSHALL

Bland, Larry, ed. *George C. Marshall: Interviews and Reminiscences for Forrest C. Pogue.* Revised edition with an Introduction by Pogue. Lexington, VA: George C. Marshall Research Foundation, 1991.

Bowers, Thomas A. *A Tonic to My Spirit: George Catlett Marshall and the American Red Cross,* Leesburg, VA: George C. Marshall International Center, 2019.

Cray, Ed. *General of the Army: George C. Marshall, Soldier and Statesman.* New York: Cooper Square Press, 2000.

Ferrell, Robert H., ed. *George C. Marshall.* Volume XV of *The American Secretaries of State and Their Diplomacy,* eds. Ferrell and Samuel Flagg Bemis, New York: Cooper Square, 1966.

Groom, Winston. *The Generals: Patton, MacArthur, Marshall and the Winning of World War II.* Washington DC: National Geographic, 2015.

Jeans Jr, Roger B. *The Marshall Mission to China, 1945–1947: The Letters and Diary of Col. John Hart Daughey.* Lanham, MD: Rowman & Littlefield, 2011.

Jeffers, H. Paul and Alan Axelrod. *Marshall: Lessons in Leadership*. New York: Palgrave, 2010.

Kurtz-Phelan, Daniel. *The China Mission: George Marshall's Unfinished War, 1945–1946*. New York: W.W. Norton, 2018.

Lubetkin, Wendy. *George Marshall*. New York: Chelsea House Publishers, 1989.

Machado, Barry. *The Education of an American Statesman*. In progress.

Marshall, George C. *Memoirs of My Service in the World War 1917–1918*. Boston: Houghton Mifflin, 1976.

Marshall, Katherine Tupper. *Together: Annals of an Army Wife*. New York: Tupper & Love, and Castleton NY: IBT Hamilton, 1946.

McCarthy, Joseph R. *America's Retreat from Victory: The Story of George Catlett Marshall*. Boston: The Americanist Library, 1951.

Millett, Allan R. "George C. Marshall, Secretary of Defense 1950–1951." *The Magazine of the George C. Marshall Foundation*, Summer 2019, pp. 20–25. See also his two-volume *The War for Korea*.

Parrish, Thomas. *Roosevelt and Marshall: Partners in Politics and War—The Personal Story*. New York: William Morrow, 1989.

Payne, Robert. *The Marshall Story: A Biography of General George C. Marshall*. New York: Prentice-Hall, 1951.

Pogue, Forrest C. *George C. Marshall: Statesman, 1945–1959*. New York: Penguin Books, 1989.

———. *George C. Marshall: Education of a General, 1880–1939*. New York: Viking, 1963.

Pops, Gerald M. *Ethical Leadership in Turbulent Times: Modeling the Public Career of George C. Marshall*. Lanham, MD: Lexington Books, 2009.

Roll, David L. *George Marshall: Defender of the Republic*. New York: Dutton Caliber, 2019.

Stoler, Mark A. *George C. Marshall: Soldier-Statesman of the American Century*. New York: Twayne Publishers, 1989.

Stoler, Mark A., ed. *The Papers of George Catlett Marshall*, Volume 7, "The Man of the Age" October 1, 1949–October 16, 1959. Baltimore: The Johns Hopkins University Press, 2016.

Taaffe, Stephen R. *Marshall and His Generals: U.S. Army Commanders in World War II*. Lawrence, KS: Kansas University Press, 2011.

Thompson, Rachel Yarnell. *Marshall: A Statesman in the Crucible of War*. Leesburg, VA: George C. Marshall International Center, 2014.

Uldrich, Jack. *Soldier, Statesman, Peacemaker: Leadership Lessons from George C. Marshall*. New York: Amacom, 2005.

Unger, Debi and Irwin. With Stanley Hirshson. *George Marshall: A Biography*. New York: HarperCollins, 2014.

The Words of George C. Marshall. Lexington, VA: The George C. Marshall Foundation, 2014.

MEMOIRS, AUTOBIOGRAPHIES, AND EYEWITNESS ACCOUNTS

Abramson, Rudy. *Spanning the Century: The Life of Averell Harriman, 1891–1986*. New York: William Morrow, 1992.

Acheson, Dean. *Present at the Creation: My Years in the State Department*. London: Hamish Hamilton, 1969.

Acheson, Dean. *The Korean War*. New York: Norton, 1971.

Appleman, Roy E. *Ridgway Duels for Korea*. College Station, TX: Texas A&M University, 1990.

Beisner, Robert L. *Dean Acheson: A Life in the Cold War*. New York: Oxford University Press, 2006.

Bohlen, Charles E. *Witness to History, 1929–1969*. New York: Norton, 1973.

Chace, James. *Acheson: The Secretary of State Who Created the American World*. New York: Simon & Schuster, 1998.

Ferrell, Robert H., ed. *The Autobiography of Harry S. Truman.* Boulder, CO: Colorado Associated University Press, 1980.

Ferrell, Robert H., ed. *Off the Record: The Private Papers of Harry S. Truman.* New York: Harper & Row, 1980.

Ferrell, Robert H., ed. *The Eisenhower Diaries.* New York: W.W. Norton, 1981.

Kennan, George F. *Memoirs, 1950–1953.* Boston: Little Brown, 1972.

MacArthur, Douglas. *Reminiscences.* New York: McGraw-Hill, 1964.

McCullough, David. *Truman.* New York: Simon & Schuster, 1992.

McLellan, David S. *Dean Acheson: The State Department Years.* New York: Dodd, Mead, 1976.

Ridgway, Matthew B. *The Korean War.* New York: Doubleday, 1967.

Thompson, Nicolas. *The Hawk and the Dove: Paul Nitze, George Kennan, and the History of the Cold War.* New York: Henry Holt, 2009.

Truman, Harry S. *Years of Trial and Hope, 1946–52.* Volume 2: of *Memoirs by Harry S. Truman.* Garden City, NY: Doubleday & Company, 1956.

SECONDARY SOURCES

Ambrose, Stephen E. *Eisenhower: Soldier and President.* New York: Simon & Schuster, 1990.

Armstrong, Charles K. *Tyranny of the Weak: North Korea and the World, 1950–1992.* Ithaca: Cornell University Press, 2013.

Beevor, Antony and Artemis Cooper. *Paris: After the Liberation, 1944–1949.* Revised edition. New York: Penguin Press, 2004.

Behrman, Greg. *The Most Noble Adventure: The Marshall Plan and How America Helped Rebuild Europe.* New York: Free Press, 2007.

Betts, Richard K. *Soldiers, Statesmen, and Cold War Crises.* Cambridge, MA: Harvard University Press, 1977.

Blair, Clay. *The Forgotten War: America in Korea, 1950–1953.* New York: Doubleday, 1987.

Borklund, Carl W. *Men of the Pentagon: From Forrestal to McNamara.* New York: Frederick A. Praeger, 1966.

———. *The Department of Defense.* New York: Frederick A. Praeger, 1968.

Brands, H.W. *The General vs. the President: MacArthur and Truman at the Brink of Nuclear War.* New York: Doubleday, 2016.

Coakley, Robert W. *Highlights of Mobilization Korean War.* Washington DC: Office of the Chief of Military History. Department of the Army, March 10, 1959.

Condit, Doris M. *The Test of War, 1950–1953.* Vol. 2 of *History of the Office of the Secretary of Defense*, ed. Alfred Goldberg Washington DC: Historical Office, Office of the Secretary of Defense, 1984.

Fehrenbach, T.R. *This Kind of War: The Classic Korean War History.* Washington DC: Brassey's, 1963.

Fontaine, André. *History of the Cold War. From the Korean War to the Present.* New York: Vantage Books, 1969.

Goodwin, Doris Kearns. *No Ordinary Time: Franklin and Elinor Roosevelt: The Home Front in World War II.* New York: Simon & Schuster, 1994.

Halberstam, David. *The Coldest Winter: America and the Korean War.* New York: Hyperion, 2007.

———. *The Fifties.* New York: Villard/Random House, 1993.

Hanley, Charles J. *Ghost Flames: Life and Death in a Hidden War, Korea 1950-1953.* New York: PublicAffairs, 2020.

———. *The Bridge at No Gun Ri: A Hidden Nightmare from the Korean War.* Henry Holt and Co., 2001.

Hitchcock, William I. *The Age of Eisenhower: America and the World in the 1950s.* New York: Simon & Schuster, 2018.

Hoyt, Edwin P. *On to the Yalu*. New York: Stein and Day, 1984.

Huntington, Samuel P. *The Soldier and the State: The Theory and Politics of Civil-Military Relations*. Cambridge, MA: Belknap Press of Harvard University, 1957.

Isaacson, Walter and Evan Thomas. *The Wise Men: Six Friends and the World They Made*. New York: A Touchstone Book, Simon & Schuster, 1986.

Jager, Sheila Miyoshi. *Brothers at War: The Unending Conflict in Korea*. New York: W.W. Norton, 2013.

James, D. Clayton. *The Years of MacArthur: Triumph and Disaster 1945–1964*. Volume 3. Boston: Houghton Mifflin, 1985.

James, D. Clayton with Anne Sharp Wells. *Refighting the Last War: Command and Crisis in Korea 1950–1953*. New York: The Free Press, 1993.

Judt, Tony. *Postwar: A History of Europe Since 1945*. New York: Penguin Press, 2005.

Kaufman, Burton I. *The Korean Conflict*. Westport, CT: Greenwood, 1999.

Kintner, William R. *Forging a New Sword: A Study of the Department of Defense*. New York: Harper & Brothers, 1958.

Lacy, James. *The Washingtonian War: FDR's Inner Circle and the Politics of Power that Won World War II*. New York: Bantam Books, 2019.

Lankov, Andrei. *The Real North Korea: Life and Politics in the Failed Stalinist Utopia*. New York: Oxford University Press USA, 2013.

Leary, William M., ed. *MacArthur and the American Century*. Lincoln: University of Nebraska Press, 2001.

Perry, Mark. *The Most Dangerous Man in America: The Making of Douglas MacArthur*. New York: Basic Books, 2014.

Machado, Barry. *In Search of a Usable Past: The Marshall Plan and Postwar Reconstruction Today*. Lexington, VA: George C. Marshall Foundation, 2007.

Manchester, William. *American Caesar: Douglas MacArthur 1880–1964*. Boston: Little Brown, 1978.

Millett, Allan. *The War for Korea*, two volumes. Lawrence: Kansas University Press, nd.

Mills, Nicolaus. *Winning the Peace: The Marshall Plan and America's Coming of Age as a Superpower*. New York: John Wiley & Sons, 2008.

Mossman, Billy C. *Ebb and Flow: November 1950–July 1951*. Washington DC: Office of the Chief of Military History. United States Army, 1972.

Poole, Walter S. *The History of the Joint Chiefs of Staff*, Volume IV 1950–1952. Printed December 1979. Marshall Library Xerox 2575 NATO, Verifax 1605.

Rearden, Steven L. *The Formative Years 1947–1950*. Volume 1 of *History of the Office of the Secretary and Defense*, ed. Alfred Goldberg. Washington DC: Historical Office, Office of the Secretary of Defense, 1984.

Reeves, Thomas C. *The Life and Times of Joe McCarthy*. New York: Stein & Day, 1983.

Sandler, Stanley. *The Korean War: No Victors, No Vanquished*. Lexington, KY: University of Kentucky Press, 1999.

Schnabel, James F. *Policy and Direction: The First Year*. Washington DC: Office of the Chief of Military History United States Army, 1972.

Settle, Frank A., Jr. *General George C. Marshall and the Atomic Bomb*. Santa Barbara, CA: Praeger, 2016.

Sides, Hampton. *On Desperate Ground: The Marines at the Reservoir, the Korean War's Greatest Battle*. New York: Doubleday, 2018.

Spanier, John W. *The Truman–MacArthur Controversy and the Korean War*. Cambridge, MA: Belknap Press of the Harvard University Press, 1959.

Steil, Benn. *The Marshall Plan: Dawn of the Cold War*. NY: Simon & Schuster, 2018.

Stueck, William. *The Korean War: An International History.* Princeton: Princeton University Press, 1995.

Taylor, William. *Every Citizen a Soldier: The Campaign for Universal Military Training after World War II.* College Station: Texas A&M, 2014.

Thompson, Wayne C. *The Political Odyssey of Herbert Wehner.* Boulder, CO: Westview Press, 1993.

———. *In the Eye of the Storm: Kurt Riezler and the Crises of Modern Germany.* Iowa City: University of Iowa Press, 1980.

———. *Nordic, Central, & Southeastern Europe 2019–20.* The World Today Series. Lanham, MD: Rowman & Littlefield, 2019.

———. *Western Europe 2019–20.* The World Today Series. Lanham, MD: Rowman & Littlefield, 2019.

Toland, John. *In Mortal Combat: Korea 1950–1953.* New York: William Morrow, 1991.

Trask, Roger R. and Alfred Goldbert. *The Department of Defense 1947–1997: Organization and Leaders.* Washington DC: Historical Office, Office of the Secretary of Defense, 1997.

Weintraub, Stanley. *15 Stars: Eisenhower, MacArthur, Marshall: Three Generals Who Saved the American Century.* New York: Free Press, 2007.

Wilkinson, Mark, ed. *The Korean War at Fifty: International Perspectives.* Lexington, VA: Department of History, VMI, 2004.

Zobel, James. *MacArthur: The Supreme Commander at War in the Pacific.* Mechanicsburg, PA: Stackpole Books, 2015

NEWSPAPERS, MAGAZINES, ETC.

"ABCs of the Big Debate," *U.S. News & World Report*, May 18, 1951.

Chicago Sun-Times, September 17, 1950. Marshall Library Scrapbook Box 214.

"Defense Chief's Basic Plan," *U.S. News & World Report,* December 29, 1950.

Hearing Before the Committee on Armed Services United States Senate, September 19, 1950.

"How Long is an Afternoon," *New York Daily News,* June 9, 1951.

"Inside Story of Joint Chiefs of Staff," *U.S. News & World Report,* May 18, 1951.

"The MacArthur Hearing," May 14, 1951.

"Marshall to Allies: Put up!" *New York Post,* September 22, 1950.

Millett, Allan R. "Korean War," *Britannica Online Encyclopedia.* https://www.britannica.com/event/Korean-War.

New York Post, November 27, 1950.

New York Times, November 25, 1950.

New York Times, March 22, 1951.

New York Times, April 15, 2018.

New York Times, December 1, 2019.

Newsweek, April 23, 1951.

"Prepare for 10 Years of Tension: An Interview with George C. Marshall," *U.S. News & World Report,* April 13, 1951.

Sunday Oregonian, September 17, 1950. Marshall Library, Scrapbook box 214.

Time, May 14, 1951.

"Toughness and Restraint at Defense," *The New York Times,* January 13, 2017.

"Truman vs MacArthur: Blow by Blow," *U.S. News & World Report,* April 20, 1951.

"Trusted Pilot at the Helm," *Phoenix Republic,* September 18, 1950. Marshall Library, Scrapbook box 214.

Washington Post, November 25, 1950.

Website of the George C. Marshall Foundation, Library and Museum in Lexington, Virginia. https://www.marshallfoundation.org/.

Index

ABOUT THE AUTHOR

PROFESSOR WAYNE C. THOMPSON TAUGHT POLITICS AT THE VIRGINIA Military Institute and Washington and Lee University. He received his doctorate from Claremont Graduate University in Claremont, California. He did further graduate study at the universities of Göttingen, Paris/Sorbonne, and Freiburg im Breisgau, where he was subsequently a guest professor. He served as a scholar-in-residence at the German Bundestag and as a Fulbright professor in Estonia. He was a visiting professor at the Air War College in Montgomery, Alabama. In 2001, he had a second Fulbright professorship at the College of Europe in Bruges, Belgium, and continued for seven years to teach at the Bruges and Warsaw campuses of that graduate institution. He also had a visiting professorship at the American University in Bulgaria. He has authored, coauthored or edited eleven books. He served as the series editor for the *World Today Series*, published by Rowman & Littlefield in Lanham, Maryland.

www.ingramcontent.com/pod-product-compliance
Lightning Source LLC
Chambersburg PA
CBHW070352090426
42733CB00009B/1383